Burton Harrison

A Virginia Cousin and Bar Harbor Tales

Burton Harrison

A Virginia Cousin and Bar Harbor Tales

ISBN/EAN: 9783744717526

Printed in Europe, USA, Canada, Australia, Japan

Cover: Foto ©Thomas Meinert / pixelio.de

More available books at **www.hansebooks.com**

A Virginia Cousin & Bar Harbor Tales

By
Mrs Burton Harrison

VT CRESCIT

M D CCC XCV
Lamson Wolffe and Co
Boston and New York

Note by the Author

THE little story "A Virginia Cousin," here put into print for the first time, is in some sort a tribute offered by a long-exiled child of the South to her native soil.   It is also a transcript of certain phases of that life in the metropolis which has been pooh-poohed by some critics as trivially undeserving of a chronicler, but fortunate hitherto in finding a few readers willing to concede as much humanity to the "heroine in satin" as to the "confidante in linen."

Of the other contents of this volume, "Out of Season" made its first appearance some time ago in *Two Tales*, and "On Frenchman's Bay" was published in *The Cosmopolitan Magazine*.

C. C. H.

NEW YORK,
   November, 1895

A Virginia Cousin

Chapter I

M R. Theodore Vance Townsend **A Vir-** awoke to the light of a spring morn- *ginia* ing in New York, feeling at odds with *Cousin* the world. The cause for this state of variance with existing circumstances was not at sight apparent. He was young, good-looking, well-born, well-mannered, and, to support these claims to favorable consideration, had come into the fortunes of a father and two maiden aunts,—a piece of luck that had, however, not secured for him the unqualified approbation of his fellow-citizens.

Joined to the fact that, upon first leaving college, some years before, he had led a few *cotillons* at New York balls, his wealth and leisure had brought upon Townsend the reproach of the metropolitan press to the extent that nothing short of his committing suicide would have induced it to look upon anything he did as in earnest.

[*3*]

With an inherited love of letters, he had dabbled in literature so far as to write and publish a book of verse, of fair merit, which, however, had been received with tumultuous rhapsodies of satire by the professional critics. The style and title of "Laureate of the 400," applied in this connection, had indeed clung to him and made life hateful in his sight. To escape it and the other rubs of unoccupied solvency, he had made many journeys into foreign countries, had gone around the globe, and, in due course, had always come to the surface in New York again, with a sort of doglike attachment to the place of his birth that would not wear away.

Of the society he was familiar with, Vance was profoundly weary. Of domestic ties, he had only a sister, married to a rich banker, and in possession of a fine new house, whose tapestries and electric lighting occupied all her thoughts and conversation that could be spared for things indoors. Away from home, Mrs. Clifton was continually on the wing, attending to the demands of philanthropy or charity, and to cultivation of the brain in

classes of women of incomes equal to her
own. Whenever her brother dined with
her, she entertained him with a voluble
flow of conversation about these women
and their affairs, never failing, however, to
exhibit her true sisterly feeling by telling
Vance that she could not see why in the
world he did not marry Kitty Ainger and
settle down.

By dint of much iteration, this suggestion of Kitty Ainger as a wife had come
to take languid possession of the young
man's brain. Besides, he liked Miss Ainger as well as admired her, and was perhaps more content in her company than
in that of anybody else he knew.

On the spring morning in question, he
had awaked in a flood of sunshine and
fresh air that poured through the open
windows of his room. His cold bath, his
simple breakfast, his ride in the Park,
brought his sensations of physical well-
being to a point that almost excited his
spirits to strike a balance of youthful cheer-
fulness. He forgot his oppressive belongings, the obloquy they had conferred upon
him in the minds of men who make pub-

lic opinion about others as citizens, his unreasonable stagnation of ambition.

As he cantered along the equestrian byways of the Park, and felt, without noting, the stir of new life in nature, he grew light of heart and buoyant. And as this condition increased, his thoughts crystallized around the image of Katherine Ainger. She, too, loved her morning ride; no doubt he should meet her presently. He had not seen her since Thursday of last week, when he had taken her in to dinner at Mrs. Cartwright's; and he had a vague idea she had resented him a little on that occasion. Her talk had been a trifle baffling, her eyes evasive. But she had worn a stunning gown, and was by all odds the best-looking woman of the lot. How well she sat at table, by the way! What an admirable figure for a man who would be forced to entertain, to place at the head of his board in perpetuity!

Their families, too, had always known each other. And she was so uncommonly level-headed and sensible! Agreeable, too; no whims, no fancies. He had never heard of her being ill for a day. As to temper and disposition, they matched all A Vir- the rest. She had never flirted; and, mar- *ginia* rying at twenty-six a husband of twenty- *Cousin* nine, she would give him no possible anxiety on that score.

Yes, his sister was right; everybody was right. Miss Ainger was the mate designed for him by heaven; and he had been a fool to dawdle so long in making up his mind to accept the fact.

As the sunshine warmed him, and his horse forged along with a beautiful even stride beneath him, Vance worked up to a degree of enthusiasm he had not felt since he played on a winning football eleven in a college game. That very day he would seek her and ask her to be his wife. They would be married as soon as she was willing, and would go away in the yacht somewhere and learn to love each other. He would have an aim, a home, a stake in the community. At thirty years of age, he should be found no longer in dalliance with time to make it pass away.

Vance, enamored of these visions, finished the circuit of the Park without see-

[7]

ing the central object of them, with whom
he had resolved to make an appointment
to receive him at home that afternoon.
He rode back to the stable where he kept
his horse, left it there, and, getting into an
elevated car, went down-town to visit his
lawyer, going with that gentleman afterwards into the stately halls of the Lawyers' Club for luncheon.

At a table near him, Vance saw, sitting
alone, a man named Crawford, whom he
had met casually and knew for a hard-
working and ambitious junior member of
the New York bar. They exchanged
nods, and Vance fancied that Crawford
looked at him with a scrutiny more close
than the occasion warranted.

"You know Crawford, then?" said
Mr. Gleason, an old friend of Vance's
father. "He began work with our firm,
but had an offer for a partnership in a year
or two, and left us. He's a tremendous
fellow to grind, but is beginning to reap
the benefit of it in making a name for himself. If that fellow had a little capital,
there is nothing he could not do, in this
community. He has never been abroad,

[*8*]

has had no pleasures of society, leads a scrupulously regular life, drinks no liquors or wines of any kind, and is in bed by twelve o'clock every night of his life. His only indulgence is to buy books, with which his lodgings overflow. We have always supposed him to be a woman-hater, until latterly, when straws seem to show that the wind blows for him from a point of sentiment. He was in the Adirondacks last summer, in camp with a friend, and I've an idea he met his fate then. After all, Vance, my dear boy, marriage is the goal man runs for, be he what he may. It will develop John Crawford, just as it would develop you, in the right direction; and I heartily wish you would tell me when you intend to succumb to the universal fate, and fall in love."

"I heartily wish I could," said Vance, with a tinge of the mockery he had that morning put aside.

At that moment, Crawford, who had finished his luncheon, passed their table, hat in hand, bowing and smiling as he did so. A waiter, jostling by, made him

loosen his hold of the hat, a rather shabby
light-brown Derby, that rolled under
Vance Townsend's feet. It was lifted
by Vance and restored to its owner before
the waiter could reach the spot; and again
Vance thought he detected a look of sig-
nificance, incomprehensible to him, in the
frank eyes Crawford turned upon him as
he expressed his thanks.

" It would have been a benefit to Crawford's friends to have accidentally put your
foot through that hat," said Mr. Gleason,
laughing. " He is accused by them of
having worn it ever since he was admitted
to the bar. But then, who thinks of
clothes, with a real man inside of them?
And no doubt the girl they say he is going
to marry will right these trifling matters
in short order."

" I like Crawford; I must see more of
him," replied Vance. " He strikes me as
the fellow to pass a pleasant evening with.
I wonder if he would come to dine with
me."

" If you bait your invitation with an
offer to show your first editions, no doubt
of it," said Mr. Gleason. " But to go

back to our conversation, Vance. When
are we to — "

"I decline to answer," interrupted the
young man, smiling, nevertheless, in such
a way that Mr. Gleason built up a whole
structure of probabilities upon that single
smile.

Yes, Vance decided, everything con-
spired to urge him toward his intended
venture that afternoon. When, about four
o'clock, he turned his steps in the direction of Miss Ainger's home, he had reached
a pitch of very respectably loverlike anxiety. He even fancied the day had been
unusually long. He caught himself spec-
ulating as to where she would be sitting in
the drawing-room, how she would look
when he laid his future in her hands.

At that moment, he allowed himself to
remember a series of occasions during the
years of their friendship, upon any one of
which he believed he might have spoken
as he now meant to speak, and that she
would have answered as he now expected
her to answer. Ah! what had he not
lost? In her gentle, equable companionship, he would have been a better, a higher,

a less discontented fellow. All the virtues, charms, desirable qualities, of this fine
and high-bred young woman, who had been
more patient, more forgiving, than he de-
served, were concentrated into one small
space of thought, like the Lord's Prayer
engraved upon a tiny coin. But even as
his foot touched the lowest step of her
father's portal, he experienced a shock of
doubt of himself and of his own stability.
He tarried; he turned away, and strolled,
whither he knew not.

In the adjoining street lived Mrs. Myrtle, an aunt of his, to whom, it must be
said, Vance rarely paid the deference considered by that excellent lady her just due.
She inhabited the brown-stone dwelling in
which, as a bride, she had gone to house-
keeping when New York society was still
within limits of visitors on foot. Not that
that made any difference to Mrs. Myrtle,
who had always kept her carriage, and had,
about twenty years back, been cited as a
leader of the metropolitan *beau monde.*

In those days, whether on wheels or
a-foot, everybody went to Mrs. Myrtle's
Thursdays. Her spacious drawing-rooms,

papered in crimson flock paper, with their massive doors and mouldings and mirror-frames and curtain-tops of ebonized wood with gold scroll decorations, their furniture in the same wood, with red satin damask coverings, had, in their time, contained the elect of good society. The pictures upon Mrs. Myrtle's walls, and the statuary scattered on pedestals about the rooms, were then quoted by the newspapers, and by those so favored as to see them, as a rare display of the highest art, accumulated by an American householder. One of the earliest affronts of many unintentionally put upon his aunt by Vance had been his contemptuous shrug of the shoulders when called upon by her, shortly after his return from his first winter spent in Italy, to view her " statuary."

Since then, Mrs. Myrtle had, little by little, come to a perception of the fact that her " art collection" was not, any more than its mistress, an object of the first importance to New York. But Vance had been always associated in her mind with the incipient stages of enlightenment, and she loved him accordingly. Her love

for Vance's sister, Mrs. Clifton, who refused to pay her tribute, and belonged to
the new " smart set," was even less.

Upon Mrs. Myrtle, Vance now resolved
to pay a long-deferred duty-call. Admitted
by an old negro butler, he was left alone
in the large darkling drawing-room, in the
shade of the crimson curtains, amid the
ghostly ranks of the statues, to ruminate
until Mrs. Myrtle should make her appearance. Little thought did he bestow upon
the duration of this ordeal. He was well
occupied, and, for once in his life, heartily
ashamed, — first, of his indecision upon the
Ainger door-steps, and, secondly, of the
fact that he had put in here to gain courage to return there.

Mrs. Myrtle's heavy tread upon her
own parquet floor aroused him from medi-
tation. His aunt was a massive lady, who
wore black velvet, with a neck-ruff of old
point-lace; who, never pretty, and no
longer pleasant to look upon, yet carried
herself with a certain ease born of assurance in her own place in life, and cultivated by many years of receiving visitors.
Her small white hand, twinkling with dia-

monds, was extended to him with some- A Vir-
thing of the grand air he remembered his ginia
mother, who was the beauty of her family, Cousin
to have possessed; and then Mrs. Myrtle,
seating herself, fixed an unsmiling gaze
upon her nephew.

"I — ah — thought I would look in and
see how you are getting on," he said, with
an attempt at jocularity.

"But it is not Thursday," she answered, cold as before. "I make it a
point to see no one except on Thursday,
or after five. And it is not yet after
five."

Townsend, who could not dispute this
fact, was at a loss how to go on. But
Mrs. Myrtle, having put things upon the
right footing, launched at once into an ex-
position of her grievances against him, his
sister, and the ruling society of latter-day
New York.

"I am sure if any one had told your
mother and me, when we first came out,
what people were to push *us* against the
wall, and to have all New York racing
and tearing after their invitations, we
should never have believed it. It's enough

[*15*]

to make your poor mother come back from the dead, to revise Anita Clifton's visiting-list. And I suppose the next thing to hear of will be your marriage into one of these bran-new families. I must say, Theodore, although it is seldom my opinion is listened to, I *was* pleased when I heard, the other day, that you were reported engaged to Katherine Ainger. The Aingers are of our own sort; and her fortune, although it is not so important to you, will be handsome. She is one of the few girls who go much into the world who still remember to come to see me; and she has been lunching here to-day."

" Really ? " said Vance, turning over his hat in what he felt to be a most perfunctory way.

" Yes; if you or Anita Clifton had been here in the last two months, you might have found out that I have had a young lady— a Southern cousin — stopping in the house."

" A cousin of mine ? " queried the young man, indifferently.

" My first cousin's daughter, Evelyn Carlyle. You know there was a break

[*16*]

between the families about the beginning of the war, and, for one reason or another, we have hardly met since. When I went to the Hot Springs for my rheumatism last year,—you and Anita Clifton doubtless are not aware that I have been a great sufferer from rheumatism,—I stopped a night or two at Colonel Carlyle's house in Virginia, and took rather a fancy to this girl. I found out that she has a voice, and desired to cultivate it in New York, and so invited her to come on after Christmas and stay in my house."

Vance was conscious of a slight feeling of somnolence. Really, he could not be expected to care for the Virginian cousin's voice. And Aunt Myrtle had such a soporific way of drawling out her sentences! He wished she would return to the subject of her luncheon-guest, and then, perhaps, he might manage to keep awake.

"So you invited Miss Ainger to-day, to keep the young lady company?" he ventured to observe.

"If you will give me time to explain, I will tell you that Katherine Ainger and

A Vir-
ginia
Cousin

she have struck up the greatest friendship this winter, and have been together part of every day. I wish, Vance, that you could bring yourself to extend some attention to your mother's first cousin's child. From Anita Clifton I expect nothing — absolutely nothing. Not belonging to the ' smart set,' whatever that may be, I make no demands upon Anita Clifton. But you, Vance, have not yet shown that you are absolutely heartless. When Eve goes home, as she soon will, it would be gratifying to have her able to say you had recognized her existence."

" I will leave a card for the young lady in the hall," he said, awkwardly; "and perhaps she would allow me to order some flowers for her. Just now, Aunt Myrtle, I have an engagement, and I must really be going on."

He had risen to his feet, and Mrs. Myrtle was about shaping a last arrow to aim at him, when the door opened, and a girl came into the room.

" Oh! Cousin Augusta," she said, in the most outspoken manner, a slight

Southern accent marking some of the *A Vir-* syllables enunciated in a remarkably sweet *ginia* voice, "I have been taking your Dandie *Cousin* Dinmont for a walk, and he has been such a good, obedient dear, you must give him two lumps of sugar when he comes to tea at five o'clock."

As Mrs. Myrtle performed the ceremony of introduction between them, Vance became conscious that he was in the presence of one of the most radiantly pretty young persons who had ever crossed the line of his languid vision. Equipped in a tailor-made frock of gray serge, a black hat with many rampant plumes upon her red-brown hair, a boa of black ostrich feathers curling around her pearly throat and caressing the rosiest of cheeks, his Cousin Eve surveyed him with as much indifference as if he had been the veriest casual met in a crowd in Fifth Avenue. Two fingers of a tiny gloved hand were bestowed on him in recognition of their relationship, after which she resumed her interrupted talk about the dog.

"You understand that Mr. Townsend

[*19*]

is a relative, my dear?" asked Mrs. Myrtle, in her rocking-horse manner. "You
have heard me speak of him?"

"Yes; oh, yes, certainly," Eve said,
with preoccupation. "But to us Vir-
ginians a cousin means either very much
— or very, very little."

"The presumption, then, is against
me?" he asked, determined not to be
subdued.

"Is it? I had not thought," she answered, hardly looking in his direction.
Vance took the hint and his departure.
When again out of doors, he straightened
himself, and walked with a firmer, more
determined tread, conscious of a little
tingling in his veins on the whole not disagreeable. In this mood, he reached the
corner of the street in which dwelt Miss
Ainger, and was very near indeed to passing it, but, recovering himself with a start,
turned westward from the Avenue, and
again sought the house from which he had
gone irresolute a little while before.

The door was opened for him by a servant, who did not know "for sure," but
"rather thought" Miss Ainger was in the

drawing-room. While following the man across a wide hall, Vance espied, lying up- on a chair, a man's hat — not the conven- tional high black hat of the afternoon caller, but a rusty brown "pot" hat, of an unobtrusive pattern.

"Humph! the piano-tuner, no doubt," he said to himself, and simultaneously re-called the fact that he had seen the object in question, or its twin brother, that same day. Before the footman could put his hand upon the knob of the drawing-room door, it opened, and the owner of the hat came out. It was indeed Crawford, dressed in morning tweeds, as Vance had seen him at luncheon in the Lawyers' Club, his plain, strong face illuminated with an expression Vance knew nothing akin to, and therefore did not interpret.

But Vance did know Miss Ainger for an independent in her set, a girl who struck out for herself to find clever and compan-ionable people with whom to fraternize; and he was accordingly not surprised to meet Crawford here as a visitor. As once before that day, the two men exchanged silent nods, and parted. Vance found

[21]

Miss Ainger caressing with dainty finger-tips a large bunch of fresh violets that lay in her lap and filled the room with fragrance.

Kitty Ainger, a daughter of New York, calm, reserved, temperamentally serious, fond of argument upon high themes, cultivated in minor points to a fastidious degree, handsome in a sculptural way, had always seemed to him lacking in the one grace of womanly tenderness he vaguely felt to be of vast moment in a young man's choice for a wife.

To-day, as she greeted him, her manner was gentle and gracious to perfection. Perhaps it so appeared in contrast to that of the fair Phyllida who had flouted him in his Aunt Myrtle's drawing-room; perhaps Kitty was really glad of this first occasion in many days when they were alone together, undisturbed.

The thought caused a wave of excitement to rise in the suitor's veins. He wondered how he could have held back, an hour before, when upon the threshold of such an opportunity. But then, had he made appearance, no doubt there would

have been other visitors, — Crawford, for A Vir-
instance, whom Miss Ainger was plainly ginia
taking by the hand, to lead into society, as Cousin
clever girls will do when they find an unknown clever man; Crawford, who did
not know enough of conventionality to
put on a black coat when he called on a
girl in the afternoon; Crawford, poor and
plain, a man's man, whom the Ainger family no doubt regarded as one of Kitty's
freaks. Yes, Crawford would have been
a decided interruption to this *tête-à-tête.*

Now, there was an open sea before
Vance, and he had only to launch the
boat, so long delayed, a craft he at last
candidly believed to be freighted with the
best hopes of his life. They talked for
awhile upon impersonal subjects — Kitty
exerting herself, he could see, to be agreeable and sympathetic with her visitor. In
the progress of this conversation, he took
note with satisfaction of the artistic ele-
gance of her dress (of the exact color of
the Peach Blow Vase, he said to himself,
searching for a simile in tint), with sleeves
of sheenful velvet, and a silken train that
lay upon the rug. Her long, white fin-

gers, playing with the violets, wore no
rings. Her slim figure, her braids of pale
brown hair, her calm, gray eyes, attracted
him as never before, with their girlish and
yet womanly composure.

"Why have you never told me," he
said abruptly, "of your friendship with
that little witch of a Virginia cousin of
mine who has been staying with Mrs.
Myrtle this winter?"

"If you wish me to tell you the truth,
it was because she asked me never to do
so," replied Kitty, coloring a little. "You
have met her?" she added eagerly.

"Yes, to-day; a little while ago, when
I called upon my aunt. But how could
she know of me? What reason was
there for her to avoid me?"

"Evelyn is an impulsive creature," was
the answer; and now the blood rushed into
Kitty's cheek, and she was silent.

"Impulsive, yes; but how could she
resent a man she had never seen; who
had not had the smallest opportunity to
prove whether or not he was obnoxious to
her? That is quite too ridiculous, I

[*24*]

think. You, who have so much sense, *A Vir-* character, judgment, why could not you *ginia* exercise your influence over this very pro- *Cousin* vincial little person, and teach her that a prejudice is, of all things, petty?"

"She is not a provincial little person," said Kitty, with spirit. "And she does not merit that patronizing tone of yours."

"If *you* take her under your wing, she is perfection," he answered lightly, as if the subject were no longer of value for discussion. "But before we begin to differ about her, only tell me if it is my Aunt Myrtle's objection to me as a type that my truculent Cousin Eve has inherited?"

"I hardly think so. Please ask me no questions," the girl said, uncomfortable with blushing.

"As you like. It is veiled in mystery," he said, rather piqued. "At least, you won't mind informing me if she got any of her ideas of me from you. No, that is hardly fair. I will alter it. Did you and she ever speak of me together?"

"What if I tell you yes, and that, every

time we met?" exclaimed Miss Ainger, plucking up courage when thus driven into a corner.

To her surprise and dismay, Vance took this admission quite otherwise than she had meant it. In Eve's attitude toward him, he thought he read a girlish jealousy of the object preoccupying the affections of her friend.

"I see. I understand," he said, with a gleam in his eyes she had not seen there in all of their acquaintance. Until now, the hearth-rug had been between them. With an animation quite foreign to him, he crossed it, and leaned down to take her hands. At once, Kitty, withdrawing from his grasp, rose to her feet and faced him.

"I think there is some great mistake," she said, very quietly. As Vance gazed at her, he became aware that he had until now never seen the true Kitty Ainger, and that her face was beautiful.

"You repulse me? You have never cared for me?" he said, fiercely.

A wave of color came upon her cheeks, and her eyes dropped before his to the violets in her hand.

"I must tell you," she said, after a *A Vir-*
pause, during which both thought of many *ginia*
things stretching back through many years, *Cousin*
"that I have just promised to marry Mr.
Crawford."

Chapter II

THE day of Miss Ainger's marriage
with Crawford, which took place in
New York, a month later than the events
heretofore recorded, found Vance Townsend on horseback in Virginia, following,
with no especial purpose, a highway that
crosses the Blue Ridge Mountains to
descend sharply into the valley of the
Shenandoah.

Before leaving home, he had acquitted
himself of conventional duty to the bride
by ordering to be sent to her the finest
antique vase of his collection, — a gem
of carved metal that Cellini might have
signed, — filled with boughs of white lilac,
his card and best wishes accompanying it.
Then, with a heart overburdened, as he
fancied, with regretful self-reproach, he
had turned his back upon the chief might-
have-been of his experience.

Katherine, who had, in fact, passed
many days in her paternal mansion un-

[28]

sought by him, was now invested with a
veil of tender sentiment. In his waist-
coat pocket he carried an unfinished poem,
addressed to her, — or to an idealized ver-
sion of Miss Ainger, — which, at intervals
on his journey, he would take out and pol-
ish and shape with assiduity, forgetting
sometimes to sigh over it in his zeal for
metrical construction.

The morning of the day that was to see
the prize he had lost become definitely
another's beheld Vance bargaining with a
farmer — a former cavalryman in the
Confederate service — to ride one of the
two horses he had shipped by train from
New York, and serve as guide in the war-
harried region through which he desired
to pass.

The process was a simple one, the sum
negligently offered for his services for a
day sufficing to cover the expenses of ex-
corporal Claggett for a fortnight, and leave
a margin to fill his pipe with. Therefore,
the rusty squire in attendance (to whom
the treat of bestriding a steed like this
would have been requital all-sufficient),
the riders left the village that had shel-

tered Townsend for the night, and at once
set out to ascend a long and toilsome hill,
giving views on every side of an enchanting prospect.

"I don't mean to appear boastful, suh,"
observed Mr. Claggett, modestly, "an' I
ain't travelled much myself out o' this
State, but I 've heerd people say this 'ere
view beats creation."

"It is very fine, certainly, Claggett,"
replied Vance, halting to look back at the
wide expanse of hill and valley mantled
with springing green, the far-off, grassy
heights serving as pasture for sheep and
cows, and scattered with limestone boul-
ders, against which redbud and dogwood
in blossom made brilliant patches; with
mountains beyond, above, everywhere, and
all of that exquisite, velvet-textured shade
of blue, so soft and melting it seems to
invite caress.

"By Jove! It is well named the Blue
Ridge," Vance went on, approvingly.

"Jest there, Mr. Townsend, in that
very spot where the old red cow's a-
munchin' in the grass, was where Pelham
stood when his artillery let fly at them

plucky Yankee cavalry that was behind A Vir-
the stone wall firin' like fury at our ginia
Confeds." Cousin

"And who was Pelham?" asked the
visitor, with interest.

"Never heard o' Pelham? Well, I
would n't 'a' thought it," was the compas-
sionate answer. "Why, suh, he was a
boy, — major of artillery — nuthin' but a
boy, — an' they killed him early in the
war. But he 'd the skill an' the sense of
an old general; an' there wornt no risk to
himself he 'd stop at in a fight. He 'd just
swipe vict'ry, every time, suh, Pelham
would; an' he was the pride an' idol of
our army. Thar! them johnny-jump-ups
are growin' where his gun stood, an' he
rammin' charges into it with his own hand,
when he sent that murderin' volley that
made batterin'-rams out o' the stones o'
the wall here, an' druv the poor Yankees
behind it into Kingdom Come. Things
look different to me, suh, now. I was a
youngster, then, run mad to git into any
kind o' fightin'; but I 've got sons o' my
own now, an' I can't somehow see the
pints in all that killin' we did in our war,

[*31*]

like I used to. But I can't think o' fellers like Pelham without wantin' to be in it again, suh.

"Why, at Snicker's Gap (heard o' Snicker's Gap, Mr. Townsend?) that lad, who was commandin' Stuart's horse-artillery, charged on a squadron of cavalry that had been botherin' him with its sharp-shooters, and, with a gun that they'd dragged by hand through the undergrowth, fired a double charge of canister into their reserves. Then, suh, he charged agin, — a reg'lar thunderbolt that sally was, — picked up sev'ral prisoners an' horses, an', limberin' up his gun like wild-fire, hurried back to his first position, his men shoutin' for him all the while."

"Those were stirring days for you, Claggett," said Townsend, whose blood began to answer to the man's enthusiasm.

"Yes, Mr. Townsend, they were so; but you mustn't let me impose on you with my war stories. My present wife, suh, — a young lady I courted in King William, about the age of my oldest daughter, — she won't have me open my mouth 'bout war stories at our house. Says I

tire everybody out with my old chestnuts, *A Vir-*
suh; an' perhaps I do. The ladies like *ginia*
to do a good deal of the talkin' themselves, *Cousin*
I've noticed, Mr. Townsend."

With a subdued sigh, Claggett subsided
into silence, but not for long. The names
of Stuart and Mosby and their officers
were ever upon his lips, interspersed with
anecdote and gossip concerning the country
people whose dwellings were only occa-
sionally seen from the road. Here and
there, in the distance, chimneys behind
clumps of trees were pointed out as belonging to old inhabitants who had held
on to their homes through storm and stress
of ill-fortune since the war.

"Since you are from the Nawth, I
would like to tell you, suh, that nobody
who is anybody among our gentry ever
lived in a village. They lived to themselves, suh, an' the further away from
each other the better. If you had the
time, suh, an' were acquainted with the
families, I could show you some places
that would surprise you. An' the ladies
an' gentlemen, Mr. Townsend, of our
best old stock are as fine people as any on

God's earth, I reckon. Pity you ain't
acquainted, as I said. It would give me
pleasure to take you inside some of the
gates of our foremost residents."

Vance noted with amusement that
Claggett did not assume to be on a social
plane with the people he extolled, but had
accepted the tradition of their superiority
as part of the Virginian creed. Laughing,
he joined in the honest fellow's regret at
his ineligibility to take rank as a guest in
the neighborhood.

"Though it seems to me, Claggett, now
that I think of it, I have a kinsman somewhere hereabout. Do you know anything
of a family of Carlyles — Colonel Carlyle, I believe they call him?"

Claggett's manner underwent instant
transformation.

"Colonel Guy Carlyle, of the Hall,
suh?" he exclaimed, eagerly. "That's
in the next county, a matter of twenty or
thirty miles from here. I had the luck to
serve under the Colonel, Mr. Townsend,
and he'd know me if you spoke my name.
You'll be goin' that way, suh? We'll

strike north from Glenwood, and get there by supper-time."

"Hold on, Claggett, you'll be pouring out my coffee and asking me to take more of the Colonel's waffles, presently. Colonel Carlyle married my mother's cousin, but I fancy would not recognize my name as quickly as yours. I have certainly no grounds for venturing to offer myself as an inmate of his house."

"Beg your pardon, suh, but the Colonel'd never get over a relation ridin' so near the Hall an' not stoppin' there to sleep," persisted Claggett. "It's a thing nobody ever heard of, down this way."

"I shall have to brave tradition, then," answered Vance, indifferently.

"It's a fine old place, suh. House built by the Hessian prisoners in the Revolution, and splendid furniture. They do say there's one mirror in the big saloon that covers fourteen foot of wall, Mr. Townsend. Yanks bivouacked in that room, too, but did n't so much as crack it. An' chandeliers, all over danglers like earrings, suh. For all they ain't got such a sight o' money as they had, Miss Eve, she's got a real knack at fixin' up, an' she's travelled Nawth, an' got all the new ideas. You must 'a' met Miss Eve when she was Nawth, Mr. Townsend. Why, suh, she's the beauty o' three counties; nobody could pass *her* in a crowd, or out of it."

"I *have* met Miss Carlyle, Claggett," Vance said, growing uncomfortable at the recollection. "But only once, and for a moment. As you say, she is a beautiful young woman."

"Then you *will* stop at the Hall, suh?" pleaded his guide.

"No," said Vance, briefly. "We will go on to Glenwood, and sleep there at the inn. To-morrow, you shall show me as much of the country as I have enjoyed to-day, but I am here for travelling, and not to cultivate acquaintance, understand."

"Up yonder, on the hill-top, suh," observed Mr. Claggett, ignoring rebuke, "when we git through this little village we're comin' to (I was in a red-hot skirmish once, right in the middle of the

[*36*]

street, ahead, suh), is a tree we call the *A Vir-*
Big Poplar. It marks the junction of *ginia*
three counties, an' 'twas there George *Cousin*
Washin'ton slept, when he was on his
surveyin' tour as a boy, suh — you 've
heard of General Washin'ton up your
way, Mr. Townsend?"

"Yes, confound you," said Vance,
laughing at his sly look.

"General Lee halted at that point to
look at the country round, on his way to
Gettysburg. A great friend of Colonel
Carlyle was the General, suh; you 'll see a
fine picture of the General in the dinin'-
room at the Hall. Colonel Carlyle lost
two brothers followin' Lee into battle, suh,
but we call that an honor down here.
They do say little Miss Eve keeps the old
swords and soldier caps of them two
uncles in a sort o' altar in her chamber,
suh. Heard the news that Miss Eve 's
engaged to her cousin, Mr. Ralph Corbin,
in Wash'n't'n, suh? It 's all over the
country, I reckon. He 's a young archy-
tec', an' doin' well; but down here nobody
knows if a young lady 's engaged for sure,
till the day 's set for the weddin'."

[*37*]

At this point Vance interrupted his gar-
rulous guide to suggest that they should
seek refreshment for man and beast in the
hamlet close at hand ; and the diversion
this created turned Claggett from the
apparently inexhaustible subject of the
Carlyles.

They rode onward, the genial sun, as
it mounted higher in the heaven, serving
to irradiate, not overheat, the beautiful
earth.

From this point the road went creeping
up, by gentle degrees, to the summit of
the mountain, beyond which Shenandoah
cleft their way in twain. Traversing
Ashby's Gap, the efflorescence of the
woods, the music of many waters, the
balm of purest air, confirmed Vance's
satisfaction in his choice of an expedition.
Descending the steep grade to the river,
they crossed the classic stream upon the
most primitive of flat ferry-boats, and on
the further side passed almost at once into
a rich, agricultural country, upon a well-
kept turnpike, where the horses trotted
rapidly ahead.

Claggett, strange to say, did not resume

[*38*] .

allusions to the Carlyle family; but upon reaching a certain cross-road, he ventured an appealing glance at his employer.

" Turn to the right here, to get a short cut to Carlyle Hall, suh."

" Where does the left road take us ? " asked Vance, shortly.

" You *kin* git to Glenwood that way, Mr. Townsend. But it's a roundabout way, an' a new road, an' a pretty bad one, an' it's just in the opposite direction from Colonel — "

Vance answered him by riding to the left.

A new road, with a vengeance, and one apparently bottomless, the horses at every step plunging deeper into clinging, red-clay mud ; but the obstinacy of Vance kept him riding silently ahead, and the trooper, with a quizzical look upon his weather-beaten face, followed. Miles, traversed in this fashion, brought them into the vicinity of a small gathering of houses, at sight of which Vance spoke for the first time in an hour.

" Claggett."

" Yes, suh ? " This, deferentially.

" If I ever go back of my own free will over that infernal piece of road " — he paused for a sufficiently strong expression.

" Yes, suh? " said Claggett, expectantly.

" You may write me down an ass."

" Yes, *suh*," Claggett exclaimed, with what Vance thought a trifle too much alacrity. " Better let me go befo' you for a little piece, Mr. Townsend," added the countryman. " Just where the road slopes down to the crick, here, it 's sorter treacherous, if you don't know the best bit."

Vance, choosing to be deaf, kept in front. He traversed the creek in safety ; but, in ascending the other side, his horse plunged knee-deep into a quagmire, — throwing his rider, who arose none the worse except for a plaster of red mud, — and emerged evidently lamed.

" He 's all right, suh, excep' for a little strain," said the ex-trooper, after his experienced eye and hand had passed over Merrylad's injuries.

" We will go at once to the hotel in the village, and get quarters for the night," said Vance, ruefully. " I 've a change of clothes in that bag you carry, so I don't

mind for myself. But I would n't have
Merrylad the worse for this for anything."

"The trouble is, Mr. Townsend," answered Claggett, "that you may get quarters fit for a horse here, but you won't be
stoppin' yourself, I 'll tell you."

"Nonsense! Come along! You lead
Merrylad; I 'm glad to stretch my legs by
a walk," and the young man started off at
a good pace, plashing ever through liquid
mire, that overflowed street and so-called
sidewalk.

There was no sign of an inn of any
kind. A few dilapidated houses of the
poorest straggled on either side the street,
at the end of which they came upon a
country store and post-office combined.
Three or four mud-splashed horses hitched
to a rock; as many mud-splashed loungers
upon tilted chairs on the platform before
the door. That was all.

"Better take 'em on to old Josey's,
Charley," called out a friendly voice to
Claggett.

"Yes, old Josey will do the correct
thing by them," remarked a full-bearded,
sunburned gentleman, who, seated astride

of a mule, now came " clopping " toward them through the mud, from the opposite direction.

" I am really afraid, Mr. Townsend," Claggett said, persuasively, " that we shall be forced to go on a mile or so further, to old Josey's."

" And who in the thunder *is* old Josey?" exclaimed Vance, testily.

" Never heard o' him up Nawth, suh?" answered the trooper, with a twinkle in his eye. " He 's the big person o' this part, — an old bachelor, — Mr. Joseph Lloyd, who runs the best farms and raises the best stock in the neighborhood. The truth is, not many visitors come here, unless they are booked for Mr. Lloyd's."

" What claim have I on him, unless I can pay my night's lodging and yours? I will leave you and the lame horse here, and make my way back to-night to Glenwood."

" To get to Glenwood, you 'd have to pass over right smart of that mire we came through," said Claggett, pensively.

" Then, in Heaven's name, let us go

to Josey's," said Vance, laughing, in spite of his bad humor.

They bade farewell to the village, and went off as they had come, Vance choosing to walk, the trooper leading the lame horse.

And now, in defiance of his plight, his melancholy appearance, the accident to his favorite, Vance yielded himself to the spell of a region that became at every moment, as he advanced, more wildly beautiful. The sun, about to set, sent a flood of radiance over hills high and low, over a broken rolling country dominated by the massive shaft of Massanutton Mountain, rising like a tower above his lesser brethren. That the " mile or two further on " stretched into four or five, the young man cared not a jot. His lungs filling with crisp, invigorating air, he strode forward, and was almost sorry when the dormer-windows of an old house shrouded by locust-trees in bloom appeared upon a plateau across intervening fields.

" Now for my best cheek ! " he said to himself. " What *am* I to say to old Jo-

sephus? Ask for lodging, like the tramp
I look? Hang it! I believe I'll sleep
under the nearest haystack, rather!"

While thus absorbed, Mr. Theodore
Vance Townsend, the fine flower of various clubs, did not perceive that he was an
object of varying interest and solicitude to
three persons looking over the fence of
a pasture near-by, where cattle were
enclosed.

Two elderly gentlemen surveyed him
closely. A girl, who had tossed a glance
at him over her shoulder, seemed to find
more attraction in the Alderney heifer,
whose saucy rough tongue was at that
moment stretched out to lick salt from a
velvet palm, than in the mud-stained way-
farer.

"That's no common tramp," said one
of the gentlemen to the other. " If you
will stay here with my Lady-love, I'll
just go and investigate his case."

Vance Townsend had, perhaps, like
other mortals, known his " bad moments "
in life. But he felt that there had been
few like this, when the old gentleman,
issuing through a gate opening from the

pasture, came to him with a quick, decided step.

The younger man took off his hat.
The older did likewise. And then Vance, between a laugh and a groan, told his story, confirmed by the apparition at that moment, in the distance, of the horses and Claggett, who was himself afoot.

"Say no more, my dear fellow, say not another word," interrupted the astonished old gentleman. "My name is Lloyd, and I'm the owner of that house behind the locusts, where I'm delighted to take you in, and Charley Claggett, too. We'll find out what's the matter with your horse, quick enough. Welcome to Wheatlands, sir, and just come along with me."

Before Vance fairly knew how, he found himself in a "prophet's chamber," looking upon a sloping roof, where a martin was nesting within reach of his hand. Tapping the panes of the upper sash of his window, a branch tasselled with sweet-smelling blossoms swayed in the breeze. Outside, he had a wide and glorious view of field and mountains. Inside, he possessed a clean, if homely, bedroom, at the

door of which a soft-voiced negro woman
was already knocking, to ask for his be-
spattered garments.

Vance was delighted. When he fur-
thermore found left at his portal a tub
with a large bucket of ice-cold water from
the spring, together with his bag, he began to think that Virginia hospitality was
not to be relegated among things tradi-
tional.

The soft Virginia dusk was closing upon
the scene, when our young man, leaving
his room, went down-stairs, through a hall
hung with trophies and implements of sport,
and out of an open door upon the " front
porch," to look at the evening star hang-
ing above the mountain crest. In this
occupation he found another person indulging likewise, and in the clear gloom dis-
covered the face and figure of a young and
singularly graceful girl, who without hesitation accosted him.

" Mr. Lloyd has told us of your mis-
hap," she said, courteously. " He is con-
gratulating himself that it happened near
enough to let him help you out of it. I

hope the horse will fare as well as the
master."

" Merrylad will be all right, thank you,
so Claggett has been up to tell me. It
appears that Mr. Lloyd, in addition to his
other attractions, is a famous amateur
vet."

" You will find he has all the virtues,"
she said, laughing. At that moment, a
lamp, lighted by the servant in the hall,
sent a stream of illumination upon them.
To Townsend's utter surprise, he saw the
face of his cousin, Evelyn Carlyle.

" You ! " he heard her say, in a not too
well pleased tone; and " You ? " he
repeated, with what he felt to be not a dis-
tinguished success.

" How extraordinary that it should turn
out to be you ! " she began again, first of
the two to recover her composure. " Did
you think — were you, that is, on your
way to visit *us ?* "

" Nothing was further from my
thoughts," he answered, bluntly. " I, on
the contrary, believed myself to be going
in the opposite direction from where you
live."

"Of course," she said, somewhat
piqued. " It is impossible you should have
known that papa and I came yesterday on
a visit to dear old Cousin Josephus. I
beg your pardon if I was very rude."

" It is certainly not a welcome that
seems inspired by what I have been led
to think is Virginia cordiality," he answered, coolly.

" But I have asked your pardon, and
that 's not the way to answer me. You
might grant it, never so stiffly; and after
that, we, being thrown together this way
through no fault of either of us, might
agree to be decently civil before papa,
who can have no idea how I feel toward
— I mean what my reasons are for feeling — well, never mind what I mean,"
she ended, vexed at his immobility.

" I quite join with you in thinking it
would be very silly to take any one else
into this armed neutrality of ours. I shall
at the earliest moment, to-morrow, relieve
you of my presence. Suppose, until then,
you try to treat me as you would another
unoffending man under my circumstances."

" Yes. You are right. It would be

better, and it would not worry papa and
Cousin Josephus," she said, reflectively.
" Well, then, if you were another man, I
should begin by asking you what brought
you to Virginia. No; that would not
be at all polite, would it? I think I shall
just say nothing at all."

" Not till you let me assure you that I
came because a fellow I know told me he
had made a driving tour in this part, last
year, with his wife, and had found it
rather nice — and another reason was,
that I wanted to get away from myself."

" You are very flattering to our State,"
she said, bridling her head after a fashion
he found both comical and sweet. She
was silent a little while, then resumed,
more gently:

" I was thinking of what you last said,
and maybe I have done you an injustice.
Maybe you are to be pitied more than
blamed."

" Do you mean because I spoiled a
good suit of clothes and hurt my horse's
leg?"

" No; not that. You are clearly not
in need of sympathy. There! They are

going to ring the supper-bell, and you must go and be introduced to my father, as his cousin. He is the dearest daddy in the world, and will be sure to try to make you come to visit us at the Hall."

"Am I to understand this is a hint not to accept?"

"I *could* stay on here, you know," she said, in a businesslike way.

"You are perfectly exasperating," he exclaimed, and then the summons came to go into the house. Just before they crossed the threshold, she appeared to have undergone another change of mind. Turning back swiftly, in a voice of exceeding sweetness she breathed into his ear these words:

"Please, I am sorry. I ought not to keep forgetting, ought I, that you are a stranger within our gates, and a cousin, really?"

"Is she a coquette?" Vance began to ask himself, but was interrupted by a *sortie* of his host in search of him.

Chapter III

VANCE TOWNSEND had reckoned *A Vir-*
without his host when he made the *ginia*
declaration that he would relieve Miss *Cousin*
Carlyle of his presence the following day.
The kind owner of Wheatlands, indulgent
to every man and beast upon his premises,
had yet a way of holding on to and con-
trolling guests that none might resist.

Vance, however, did not try very hard
to resist the invitation to stay at least until
" Thursday, when the Carlyles would be
running away home." An evening spent
with the kind, simple, yet cultivated people who formed the little *coterie* at Wheatlands (there was among them a widowed
cousin with her unruly boy, and a cousin
who had been unfortunate in his invest-
ments) had, somehow, quite upset our
hero's notions upon many points.

Claggett, dismissed with a *douceur*, the
liberality of which consoled that worthy
countryman for an early reunion with

[*51*]

the lady who would not allow him to
tell stories of the war, took an affection-
ate leave of his employer. In his manner Vance detected more satisfaction in
the vindication of Virginia customs than
regret at the severance of their relation.
The little triumph Claggett might readily
have derived from the incident of the way-
farer's meeting, in spite of himself, with
his relations was heroically suppressed.
And before Townsend had turned upon
his pillow the morning after his arrival, a
telegram had gone to the town where his
luggage had been left, ordering it to be
sent by train that day.

Vance had been told that breakfast
would be at nine; and, awakened at half-
past seven by a bird on the bough in his
window, he abandoned himself to a lazy
review of his impressions of the family.
Of his Cousin Eve he had seen little more
than what has already been told. After
filling her place at a bounteous supper-
table, where the talk was chiefly absorbed
by the three gentlemen, she had vanished,
in company with the widowed cousin, and
was invisible thereafter — the men sitting

together till midnight in the large, raftered
hall, with a fire in its wide chimney, that
served the old bachelor for a general liv-
ing-room.

Vance could not remember to have seen a face of finer lines, a manner of finer courtesy, than that of his seventy-year-old host, who, in spite of the rust of desuetude in worldly ways, carried his inbred gentility where all who approached him might profit by it.

That he was a politician went without saying; and, indeed, the talk once directed in the channel of national government had kept there until they separated. On a claw-footed table holding a lamp beside Mr. Lloyd's easy chair, covered with frayed haircloth, Vance saw lying a crisp new Review of English publication, and all about were piled newspapers and magazines, while shelves displayed row upon row of the antique, tawny volumes that had made up the complete library of a country gentleman in the days of old Josephus's grandfather.

Around the hearth, coming and going with every opening of many doors, gath-

ered dogs of fine and varied breeds. One
old patriarch of a St. Bernard, who at-
tached himself particularly to the stranger, had remained close to Vance's feet,
and gravely escorted him to bed.

In his kinsman, Guy Carlyle, a handsome man of fifty odd years, who in a
military youth had been noted for deeds of
daring that rang through the army of
Northern Virginia, but had long since
resigned himself to the peaceful pursuits
of agriculture, Vance saw the origin of
Eve's rare beauty. He also became
aware that, of a large family of sons and
daughters born to the now widowed Colonel, Eve was the sole survivor; and it did
not need the expression that irradiated her
father's face when her name was touched
upon to show in what estimation she was
held by him.

The tinge of melancholy in Mr. Carlyle's manner had, however, no effect like
repression of the cordial friendliness he
extended to the newcomer. Vance had
gone to rest with a feeling that he had
conferred a genuine favor upon his two

[*54*]

elders by according to them, as he had,
his company.

Spite of these conditions of good-fel-
lowship, he awoke next morning conscious that there was one under the roof
with him who had the power (and no desire to withhold it) to make him far from
comfortable; to puzzle him, to banter
him, to pull him up with a jerk at the
moment he might feel that he was getting
reasonably ahead with her; to punish him,
it would appear, for some offence he could
not own to having committed.

It was very clear that Eve thought him
a poor fellow, mentally and morally; that,
apart from her specific grudge against him,
of nature unknown, she was not in the
least inclined to pay tribute to his position,
fashion, culture, wealth, — the appendages
of Vance Townsend's personality people
around him had always been disposed to
make so much of. In the firmament of
American society, he took himself to be
a planet of first importance. In other
lands, he had enjoyed more than a reason-
able share of social success. Why should
he here, for the first time in his life, feel

like a man coming in fancy costume to a
dinner where all the other guests wore
plain clothes?

It must be the doing of that girl. She
it was who, with a few words, a cool
glance or two that appeared to read his
soul, had brought him into this strait; and
Vance was still young enough to feel himself flame with resentment of her. Then
fell upon his mental ear the soft cadence
of her voice, asking his pardon for having
possibly misjudged him, and his anger
passed.

As from Eve he went on to think of
Kitty Ainger, now Mrs. Crawford, Vance
was surprised at the freedom from sore-
ness the reflection left upon his mind.
Mrs. Crawford, he even reflected, was
really an admirable woman — just the wife,
as everybody had said, for a rising fellow
like Crawford, who would surely reach
the top! She had shown her good sense in
taking him. Was it possible Vance had
ever thought anything else?

On a table near the bed lay the contents of a pocket emptied overnight —
among them a folded paper, inscribed with

the latest and most satisfactory draft of his verses to Kitty.   This he now seized, and, upon re-reading it, a flush that was not of tender consciousness overspread his face.   Regardless of the loss to the world of poetry, ignoring the recurrent efforts that Calliope had witnessed, he deliberately tore it up, and went to the open window prepared to scatter the tiny remnants upon a matin beeeze.

A view of wide green plains, with here and there a clump of noble trees, of soaring blue hills beyond them, all shining in the morning sun, met his eye ; and almost directly beneath his window were a couple of horses, of which one was bestridden by old Josephus, in a nankeen coat and venerable Panama hat ; the other, little more than a colt, was held by a negro and saddled for a woman's use.

"Lady-love ! Lady-love, I say ! " called out the old gentleman, in a voice of Stentor.

" Coming, coming, come ! " gaily answered somebody ; and in a moment Vance's Cousin Eve appeared.

Springing lightly upon the segment of

an enormous tree that served as horse-
block, she dropped into her saddle, and
devoted herself to subduing the juvenile
remonstrance of her steed.

With the fragments of his effusion to
Kitty Ainger still in hand, Vance felt a
curious sensation, as though the old world
had suddenly become young and beautiful
and tuneful; and then, from his ambush,
he heard Josephus say:

" I 'd half a mind to rouse up our visitor, and take him with us to see the sheep
in Six-Acre Lot. The ride before breakfast would have given him a good idea of
the way my land lies."

" O Cousin Josey, I am so thankful
you did *not!* " answered Eve, with sin-
cerity unmistakable.

" Tut, tut, my dear child," began Mr.
Lloyd, rebukingly; but Eve, who just then
succeeded in starting her colt in the right
direction, was off and away, sending back
a trill of laughter to her ancient cavalier,
who made good speed to follow her.

The new conviction of his folly in having agreed to remain under the same shel-
ter with Miss Carlyle did not prevent Mr.

Townsend from making his appearance with an excellent appetite at the breakfast- table, whither he was duly escorted by Bravo, the old dog he had found outside his bedroom door waiting to take him in charge.

With Bravo and another dog or two at heel, Vance had walked off his pique over dew-washed slopes of short, rich grass to a summit near the house, to be joined on the return by Colonel Carlyle, who had strolled out to meet him.

Breakfasts at Wheatlands were justly considered the *chefs d'œuvre* of old Josey's cook. Vance, helping himself to quickly succeeding dainties seen for the first time, cast a mental glance backward to the egg and a cup of tea that formed his accustomed meal at home. Half-way in the repast, Eve, who had been changing her habit to a pretty cotton gown, slipped into place between her father and the widow, who was pouring out the coffee.

" What! What!" said Cousin Josey, detecting her absence from a seat at his side, that would have brought her face to face with Townsend. " My Lady-love

[*59*]

desert me like that? Come back, little
runaway, and see your Cousin Vance taste
his first mouthful of a Wheatlands ham!"

Thus adjured, Eve could but take the
seat indicated; and Vance, who had determined to be no longer oppressed by so
small and pink a person, bestowed on her
an openly admiring glance that angered
her anew.

"We must leave you to Eve's mercies
this morning, Mr. Townsend," observed
their host, at the conclusion of the repast.
"Carlyle and I have promised to ride over
to the County Court to hear a case tried,
and to call on the Judge, who is an old
college chum of the Colonel's. We shall
be home to dinner at two, and you young
people must entertain each other until
then."

"Could you not manage not to show
so plainly what you feel?" asked Vance
in his cousin's little ear, as they left the
table. "Pray believe that I am not a
party to the infliction put upon you."

They had strolled bareheaded out under
the trees shading the lawn about the house.

"Shall we never have done quarrelling?"

said Eve, wearily. "Just as I think I begin to feel kindly toward you, something happens, and I break down again."

"Were we not moderately successful last night, when I assumed to be somebody else?" he asked.

"Yes; that is better. I will treat you as I would any other man stopping here — any one not of your exalted class, I mean."

"That was a quite unnecessary taunt. But I will allow it to pass if you agree for to-day — until the gentlemen return — to treat me as you would Mr. Ralph Corbin, for example."

"What do you mean?" she asked, quickly. "Ralph is the dearest, most obliging cousin I have, and I impose upon him dreadfully. If he were here, I should begin by sending him indoors to fetch my hat and parasol from the hall rack, and a new magazine I left in the window-seat, and tell him to call the dogs to come with us — What! *you* can't intend to condescend to wait upon a mere girl, a country cousin?"

He was off and back again with the articles demanded, showing no enmity in

the smile offered with them to her acceptance. But he did not at once surrender
the periodical, or until he had satisfied himself of the contents of the page held open
by a marker of beaten silver.

" You don't mind my looking at what
you read ? " he asked.

" If you like. It is some verses — *not*
what *you* would care for, in the least, but
they have given me great pleasure."

A glance showed him that his suspicion
was correct. The stanzas in question
had been written by him some months
before, and sent, unsigned, to the editor.

" Will you tell me what you fancy in
these ? " he said, with fine indifference of
manner.

" Why does one like a flower, or wor-
ship a star ? They suit me, I suppose,
and I am learning them by heart."

His own heart throbbed with a schoolboy's glee and pride. But he said nothing, and walked beside her light figure, in
the round of garden and orchard, bringing
up in the stable-yard. Here, a space
paved with grass-grown cobblestones was
bounded on three sides by frame structures,

now, in their decay, as gray and as fragile- *A Vir-*
looking as hornets' nests. *ginia*

"And the little house built of lime- *Cousin*
stone, with one window, was put up in
Colonial days, for refuge in case of an
Indian raid. Mr. Lloyd will tell you one
of his best stories, about an adventure of
his ancestor in there, when three white
men successfully resisted a band of red-
skins. Perhaps our aboriginal anecdotes
would bore you, however. If so, give us
only a little hint, and we desist. Now,
shan't we go in and see your horses?"

She lifted the latch; Vance followed her,
past stalls where the occupants gave her
immediate recognition, to those in which
his own pair were comfortably ensconced.
Merrylad, ungallant fellow, would have
none of the young lady, but at the touch
and voice of his master, turned his beautiful head sidewise to lay it upon Vance's
shoulder with affection.

"I am, at last, an illustration of the
legend, 'Some one to love me,'" he said,
laughing. "So you thought I had forsaken you, old man? Not I, my beauty.
Gently, gently, you are too demonstrative."

"I can't imagine life without horses and dogs; can you?" she said, with the quickly growing comradeship of a child. "There; I was determined that Merry-lad should let me stroke his neck!"

From the stables, whose inmates seemed to have put them upon a better footing, they passed again under the pink-blossomed arcades of an apple-orchard, to pause beside a curious indentation, like a dimple, in the turf.

"Just here," began Evelyn,—"but I shall not tell you, unless you promise to be properly impressed,—a sad fate overcame a dishonest negro servant of Mr. Lloyd's ancestor. He—the servant, I mean—was a fellow much given to acrobatic feats, and was accustomed to divert his master's guests by tumbling and turning cart-wheels. One day, he robbed old Mr. Lloyd's money-chest, and filling his pockets, went out in the orchard, and testified his glee by standing on his head."

"What happened? Evidently something of a supernatural nature."

"The earth opened, and out came a great hairy red hand," said Eve, "(I am

[*64*]

telling it to you as my nurse told it to me)
and ' cotched him by de hayde, and drawed him down.' "

" What evidence do they offer of this event ? "

" That is the thrilling part. About fifty years ago, when the present owner was just of age, some men at work in this place dug up a treasure of golden ' cob-coins,' clipped here and there to reg-ulate their value, as the custom was in olden days. And there, wedged in the earth where the gold lay scattered, was the skeleton of a man standing upon his head ! "

" Proof positive," said Vance, laughing.

" I thought I should convince you. As an actual fact, the coins brought six hun-dred dollars at the Philadelphia mint, and the money was distributed among the finders."

" Imagine how many darkeys have stolen out here, since, to work at night with pick and shovel ! I suppose that accounts for the depression of the sod."

" I myself found a George II. coin in the garden yesterday. See ! If I were to

[65]

give it to you, do you think it would bind you to continue to be 'some one else,' during the rest of your stay with us?"

He took the bit of copper she held out, wondering, as he had done the night before, whether this kindly mood meant coquetry, then deciding it was but the frolic spirit of a wholesome and untrammelled youth not to be restrained. Whatever it meant, he would profit by it. A creature so bright, so impulsive as this, his new-found cousin, was not within his ken, even if the occasional prick of her wit did keep him in an attitude of self-defence.

" Her cheeks are true apple-blossoms," he found himself murmuring, irrelevantly, as he pursued her through the tunnel of orchard boughs. " But her lips — what? Ah! bard beloved, I thank you —' Her mouth a crimson flower.' That's it. ' Her mouth a crimson flower.'"

" What are you talking about, back there?" exclaimed his guide, turning sharply to call him to account.

" Did I speak aloud? I was — ah —

[*66*]

only wondering where we are going to
bring up?"

"Do I tire you? Perhaps you are not
used to walking. Never mind; we shall
soon reach the graveyard, and then you
can sit upon the stone wall and rest."

"I think I can last to the graveyard,"
meekly said the young man, whose tramps
in the Alps and Dolomites and Rockies
had included of "broken records" not a
few.

"Now, you are laughing at me," she
said, suspiciously. "But you know I have
never heard of you except as a lounger in
clubs and a leader of *cotillons.*"

Vance thought it useless to protest.

They now reached an enclosure under
a grove of maples, where, motioning him
to sit upon a low wall tapestried with moss
and fern and creepers, she perched upon
the gnarled root of a tree, and, opening
her book, prepared to become absorbed
in it.

"Suppose you read aloud to me," he
suggested, with cunning aforethought.

"This?" she said, doubtfully, survey-

[67]

ing his verses. "Oh, no; I think not. You would hardly care for *this*. It is something quite out of your line, don't you see? The writer gives expression to a perfectly straightforward, yet eloquent, expression of a true man's true feeling, about a thing of every day. It is not only that the words are lovely and the sentiment is noble, but the measure ripples like a stream — Why, what is the matter with you? One would think you know the author."

"I am afraid, upon reflection, that I *do not* know the author," he said, drawing back into his shell.

"If you did, I should get you to thank him for me for this," she resumed. "They say authors are always disappointing to meet, after one has idealized them through their writings. But *he* would not be. No; I would trust him, through everything, to be a noble gentleman. Of course he is unworldly. I believe he lives in a remote Territory, and despises petty conventionalities of society, especially those in New York. And I think he never even heard of that dreadful 400 of yours."

Vance, smiling at her girlish nonsense, A Vir-
felt himself, nevertheless, lapped in the *ginia*
Elysium of her speech. *Cousin*

Then her mood changed to pathos, as
she told him the story of " Cousin Josey's "
single episode of love, ending in the mound
beside them, where slept the old man's
bride-betrothed of seventeen, — a ward of
his mother, — who had died of a tragic
accident, forty years agone.

" And every day, since, he has come
here. See, there are fresh wood-violets
upon her breast. And the dear old man
has never thought of such a thing as giving her a successor. Now, let us go.
There are lambs to show you, and a lot
of other things."

The passing cloud was gone from her
April face. She was again radiant, and in
some bedazzlement of mind he arose and
followed her.

Townsend's acquaintance with his Virginia cousins had, as might have been
expected, prolonged itself into a visit to
Carlyle Hall·; and he was on the eve of
departure, after a stay of two weeks in

that delightful refuge, before he realized
how much his fancy had begun to twine
around the place and its inmates.

Sentiment for the young creature who
was its ruling spirit he did not admit, other
than the natural tribute of his age and sex
to hers. Nor did he give her credit for
more than temporary feeling on any point
disconnected with her strong local attach
ments. Her father, her home, and those
she grandiosely called her " people " —
meaning, he supposed, the individuals indebted to Providence for having been born
within the limits of her State — were the
objects of Eve's warm affection.

Vance felt sure her courteous thought
of him was the result of only transmitted
consideration for a guest. So soon as he
should quit the pleasant precincts of the
Hall, he feared he must put aside his claim
to even this consideration. This condition
of affairs worried our young man more
than he cared to admit to himself. To no
one else would he have confessed that the
fortnight had been spent by him in a daily
effort to impress upon her a personality
widely different from her conception of it.

Now, at the end of his enterprise, he was conscious that he had not advanced in the endeavor; and this last evening in her company was correspondingly depressing to his *amour propre.*

They were sitting together in a window-seat of the drawing-room, looking into an old-world garden with box walks, a sun-dial, and a blaze of tulips piercing the brown mold. From the western sky, facing them, the red light was vanishing, and in the large, dim room a couple of lamps made islands of radiance in a sea of shadows. In the library, adjoining, sat the Colonel, reading, his strong, handsome head seen in profile from where they were. ♦ Sounds of evening in the country, the sweet whistle of a negro in the distance, alone broke the spell of silence brooding over the old house. Vance hesitated to further disturb it, the more so that Evelyn had been in a mood of unusual graciousness. Nor did he, in truth, feel prepared to broach the discussion of certain things he had put off until now.

"To-morrow," he said at last, with a genuine sigh, "I shall be on my way

[71]

northward, and this beautiful, restful life will be among my has-beens."

"Too restful, I'm afraid," she cried, in her brusque, schoolgirl fashion. "Your Aunt Myrtle always speaks of Virginia as nothing but a 'cure,' which she is clearly glad to have accomplished and lived down."

"It has been a cure for me in another sense. I wonder if you know what you have done for me?"

"I?"

"Yes. Don't fence with me now. For once, believe in your cousin, who is, after this, going to leave you for a long time in peace. Tell me; when I shall have gone, and that big, comfortable 'spare room' is put in order again for the next guest, shall you sometimes think of the subject of your missionary labors in the past two weeks?"

"But I have never undertaken to reform you," she said, in a vexed tone. "It is absurd for you to think I imagined myself capable of that. The best I could hope for was that your visit should pass without our coming to open conflict.

Papa could tell you I promised him to try
that this should be so."

"Then I am indebted to your father
for the modicum of personal consideration
you have vouchsafed me ? " ·

"And Cousin Josey — yes," she answered, with startling candor. "At the
same time, I must say, I like you now
better than I believed I ever could. It
makes me wish with all my heart I could
trust you."

Vance felt a sting that was not all
resentment, or all pain. The expression
of her eyes, so fearless, so intense, waked
in him a feeling that, in the moment they
had reached, he desired nothing so much
in all the world as to win this "mere
girl's" approval. The color deepened in
his face, as he said :

"And yet you have given the author of
those verses, who happens to be myself,
credit for something in which you could
place faith ? "

"You — *you* ? " she exclaimed, starting
violently. "Ah no ! Don't destroy my
ideals."

"This may be wholesome, but it is

certainly not pleasant," he said, praying Heaven for patience.

There was nothing of her customary light spirit of bravado in the manner in which, after a pause, she next spoke to him.

"I hardly know how — for the sake of others, I mean, not on my own account — to ask if it is possible you have not, in connection with me, given a thought to one who was my daily, intimate companion all of last winter."

"That!" he interrupted, with a dry laugh. "Why not arraign her for the wreck of me?"

"You understand me, I see," she said, with meaning. "Let me say this, then: that I hold a trifler with women's hearts to be the most despicable of characters. A man who is too indolent or too infirm of purpose to deny himself the pleasure he gets from watching his progress in a girl's affections is an offender the law may n't reach, but he deserves it should. That he makes his victim old before her time, in his gradual, refined disappointment of her hopes, may not count for much, in your estimation. But — but — oh! I could not have believed it of the person who wrote those verses!" *A Vir-ginia Cousin*

There were tears in her honest eyes, a tremor in her young voice. Save for these, Vance, who had walked away from her a dozen steps, would have continued to put distance between himself and this "angel at the gate."

As it was, he controlled himself sufficiently to return and say, in a hard, strained voice:

" I shall not attempt to change your estimate of me. But I am glad you have given me an opportunity to tell you that on the day I saw you first, I went directly from my aunt's house to ask Katherine Ainger to be my wife. Some day, when you are older, and know more of the world, and take broader views of poor humanity, all these things may seem to you different. Then you may, perhaps, admit that, with all my faults, I could never be such a cad as you have pictured. In the little time that we are together now, please, let us say no more about it."

He walked away, joining the Colonel,

to engage that unsuspecting gentleman in
an exhaustive discussion of politics.

Eve sat for awhile in her dusky corner,
absorbed in thought. She had decided to
say a few words to him, before he should
go, that might contribute to her relief
rather than his. But Vance gave her no
opportunity to speak any words to him,
except those of conventional farewell.
Betimes, next morning, he took leave of
his cousins; and the Virginia episode was
over.

After he had left, Eve locked herself in
her room, and gave way to a burst of
tears.

Chapter IV

IN a railway carriage that had long before *A Vir-*
left Genoa with the ultimate intention *ginia*
of getting into Rome, a girl sat, tranced *Cousin*
in satisfaction, looking from the window,
throughout an afternoon of spring. To
speed thus leisurely between succeeding
pictures of a scenery and life she seemed
to recognize from some prior state of existence — although now, in fact, seen for
the first time — was a joy sufficient to an-
nihilate fatigue.

The milk-white oxen ploughing the red
fields ; the peasant women at work amid
young vines ; the sheets of wild flowers ;
the pink and white and blue-washed villas,
with their terraces and palms and flower-
pots ; the hedges of roses, and groves of
olive and eucalyptus ; above all, the classic
names of stations, albeit placarded in a
commonplace way, — made Miss Evelyn
Carlyle, lately a passenger of a steamer

arriving at Genoa from America, turn and
twist from side to side of the carriage, and
flush and thrill with satisfaction, after a
fashion causing her father, who accom-
panied her, to rejoice that they occupied
their apartment undisturbed.

As evening closed upon the scene, she
at last consented to throw her head back
upon the cushion of the seat, and admit
she was a prey to the mortal consideration of exceeding hunger. Since leaving Genoa, a roll and some cakes of choc-
olate, only, had supplied the luncheon for
a journey of ten hours. Therefore, when
the train, stopping after dark at a little
buffet, was promptly forsaken by its passengers, Eve and her father joined the
eager throng craving refreshment at the
hands of a perspiring landlord and his
inefficient aids.

"If I could only make these fellows
understand, perhaps they would stop to
listen," said Colonel Carlyle, growing
wroth at the struggling, vociferating, jostling crowd massed in a small room,
snatching for food like hungry dogs.

"Allow me to — By Jove, it's the

Colonel!" said a voice behind him, whose possessor was trying to pass on.

"Ralph Corbin! Where did you drop from?" and, "Ralph, this is too delightful!" were the greetings received by the young man thus unexpectedly encountered.

"I am on my way from Nice to Rome to meet—er—some friends who are expected there for the Silver Wedding festivities," said he, with becoming blushes.

"I know," exclaimed Evelyn, gleefully. "I was sure they had something to do with it."

"But it's uncertain whether they have returned from Greece yet; and it's awfully jolly to meet you, anyway, Eve, and the Colonel. Here, let's get some food, and I'll go in your carriage for the rest of the way, of course. I'd not an idea you were coming out this year."

"Nor we, until a fortnight since," said Eve.

Ralph capturing a supply of bread, and fruit, and roast chicken, they made off with their booty to the train, and the evening passed in merry chat and explanation

of their plans. Evelyn, however, by no
means lost the consciousness of her advance for the first time upon Rome; and
when, after crossing the Tiber at midnight, and catching glimpses, on either
side the railway, of ruins that heralded
their vicinity to the goal of her hopes,
she was keyed to high excitement.

Ralph laughed at her disappointment as
the train ran slowly into a large, modern
station lighted by electricity, and deco-
rated with hangings of gold and crimson,
a crimson carpet spread across the platform to one of the doors of exit. When
they enquired of the *facchino* who took
their bags in charge, what great arrival
was expected, the man answered with an
indifference worthy of democratic New
York: "It is for the Silver Wedding of
their Majesties, Signor; but there are so
many Kings and Emperors and Princes in
Rome now, we have ceased to take
account of them."

"We have struck Rome at a crowded
season," said Ralph, "and I don't know
that you are going to like it overmuch. I
say, Eve, if Somebody does n't come for

another week or so, what a heaven-send
you and your father will be to me for
company !"

" That is the most cold-blooded way of making use of us to kill time with," said Eve ; but she bestowed on him a well-pleased smile. To her, Ralph had been ever a chum, — a dear, good fellow, who was the best of company. His unexpected appearance here promised to add tenfold to her pleasure, while his hopes in the affair hinted at between them had been, for some time, familiar to her in detail.

" And all this while I have never told you," he went on, in his boyish manner, " that at Nice I fell in with that swell New York cousin of yours, Vance Townsend. Not half a bad chap, if he is rather close-mouthed. Should n't wonder if he 's in Rome, now, like everybody else in this part of the world."

" Townsend?" said the Colonel, with animation. " Glad to hear there 's a chance of seeing him. Just a year — is n't it, Eve? — since he visited us at the Hall. Well, there 's no doubt we are in luck, if we meet Vance as well as you, Ralph."

"The funny part of it is," whispered the joyous Ralph to Evelyn, "some of the people we both knew in Nice put it into Townsend's head I was coming here to meet my *fiancée*. And you know, Eve, I am not engaged to her yet; her mother put us on probation for six months. The six months are out next week, though, and I don't think it would hurt Maud's mamma to hurry herself a little bit to get here, do you? How you will admire Maud's style, Evie! Her hair is dark as —" etc., etc., until Evelyn cut it short by jumping into the carriage drawn up in waiting for them.

Just now, she was not as well prepared to listen as usual. Certain feelings she had believed extinct proved themselves to have been merely dormant. Even the spectacle of Rome *en fête*, by night, its bands and fountains playing, its streets still filled with lively promenaders, did not wholly distract her from this sudden tumult of an emotion she was not prepared to define.

Constantly, during the crowded days that followed, while they drove hither and thither, attracted but provoked by the jumbling of ancient and modern in these haunts of history, she tried to persuade herself she was not ever on the alert to see somebody who did not appear. For, from among the many acquaintances and a few friends encountered in the streets of the sociable little city, Vance was persistently missing.

Ralph, however, whose sweetheart also kept her distance, proved his philosophy by devoting his days to the Carlyles; and thus, under a sky blue as the fabled Elysian fields of Virgil, the festal week went on. Wherever their Majesties of Italy and Germany passed in public, they were greeted by thoroughfares black with people, windows and balconies blazing with flags and draperies, the clash of bands and the clank of soldiery.

The coachman engaged for the service of our friends would contrive, wherever bound, to take on the way some passing show of sovereigns; and, upon a certain fair day, for no reason avowed, he drove them into the tangle of vehicles and people always seen surrounding the doors of the Quirinal Palace whenever there was a

chance to catch glimpses of royalties upon
the move. There ensconced, the saucy,
bright-eyed fellow stood up, pretended his
inability to get out of the snarl, gesticu-
lated, talked to his friends and threatened
his enemies in the crowd, while visibly
rejoicing in the opportunity to see all
likely to occur in that coveted quarter.

" Look here, cabby, if you don't move
out of this to the Baths of Caracalla in
just two minutes and a half," began Ralph,
at last, in emphatic English ; but he had
no reason to go on, as the driver, seeing
the young man's face, gathered up the
reins, and extricated himself with much
dexterity from the crowd.

Neither of his passengers noticed that
a gentleman, in a carriage just then crossing theirs, looked at them, leaned forward,
gave orders to his coachman, and at once
proceeded to follow on their tracks.

In the glorious ruin of the greatest of
temples to athletic exercise, Evelyn drew
a deep breath of delight. Nothing in
Rome, not even the Colosseum, had so
impressed her with the grandeur of by-

gone achievement in architecture as this A Vir-
wondrous pile, with its vast spaces, the ginia
gray walls breached by Time, out of Cousin
which maidenhair grew and crows were
flying — " crying to heaven for rain," as
the guide poetically explained ; the stately
columns of red porphyry grouped around
the beautiful mosaic floors; the lace-like
traceries of carven stone ; the niches and
pedestals from which marvels of old sculp-
ture had been removed; over all, the air
that is gold and balm combined !

Evelyn leaned against a column ab-
stractedly, while Ralph and her father
walked about, discussing with their guide
facts and statistics of the Thermæ. They
had indeed strolled quite out of her sight,
when a shadow on the pavement beside
her caused her to look up. If an answer
to thought be no surprise, then was not
Evelyn surprised; for the person confront-
ing her was Vance Townsend.

" I have known that you were in Rome
ever since the night you arrived," he said,
without preamble other than coldly offer-
ing her his hand. " I happened to be at

[*85*]

the station to meet an English friend, when you came out; and I saw you get into your carriage and drive away."

"Then you can hardly claim to have earned a welcome from us, now," she began to say, lightly, but found it impossible to go on, checked by the look upon his face.

"I make no pretences," he said, bitterly. "If you care to know that I have either kept you in view every day since, or else have gone for long rides into the country, where I saw nobody, it is quite true. I have done everything foolish, everything foreign to my principles and habits, to satisfy, or to get away from, the feeling the sight of you aroused in me. I wonder what you'd think, if I told you I've been wandering about pretty much ever since I parted with you, a year ago, trying to get you out of my head. Many's the letter I've written to you and destroyed. Twice I set out to see you, and once I got back into the neighborhood of your home. When I saw you in the crowd at the station here, I actually thought I was pos-

[*86*]

sessed——" He checked himself. "I beg
your pardon. I have no right to say these
things to you, I know."

"You? You?" she could only repeat,
bewildered by the meaning in his tone and
the expression of his eyes. "Is it possible that you——"

"That I fell in love with you that time
when you were holding me to account for
a thousand transgressions, committed or not
committed? Yes, it is quite possible. That
need not prevent our remaining good
friends, need it? I hope I've too much
common sense to ask you to indulge in a
discussion of these points, now; during the
past week, I've been engaged continually,
and I trust with some success, in disposing
of the last remnant of hope I may have
cherished that some day things might work
around to give me at least a chance."

"You make me very unhappy," she exclaimed.

"That is far from my wish," he said,
more gently. "Just at present you ought
to be walking on roses. There! Your
father and Corbin are coming back this

way. I want to ask you to help me to
excuse myself in your good father's sight,
if I seem unsociable."

" One word," she said, the blood flaming into her cheeks. "It is due you to know that long ago, soon after you left us, I received a letter from Katherine Crawford, — a letter that made me understand many things I had judged harshly in your conduct."

" Mrs. Crawford has been always kind to me," he answered. " And no one rejoices more than I in her present happiness."

" Yes, she is happy, — perfectly so, — and her life is full of the duties that best suit her. She says it was all planned out for her by Providence, and kept in reserve until she was fit for it."

" So runs the world away ! " he exclaimed, with a whimsical gesture.

After that, the others came, and there was much talk of the subjects naturally presenting themselves. When they moved out of the enclosure to go to the carriage, Vance walked with the Colonel, following Evelyn and Ralph.

"You will dine with us at our hotel
this evening?" said the older man, at
parting.

"I am sorry that I am engaged," Vance
answered, with appropriate courtesy, "and
that to-morrow I am off for Sicily. Some-
time, later on in your wanderings, I shall
hope to run upon you again. This is the
worst of pleasant meetings in travel, is it
not?"

When they were seated in the victoria,
he shook Evelyn's hand last.

The day was finally at hand that was to
bring Ralph's sweetheart — with her incidental father, mother, two younger sisters,
and a governess—to the quarters engaged
for them at Rome. In the young man's
enthusiasm, he did not forget to wonder
what cloud had passed over his Cousin
Evelyn's enjoyment of the place, the sights,
the season. He even consulted the Colonel
as to whether Eve might not be unduly affected by the crowded condition of the
town, and proposed for them to change to
a quieter spot. And Eve's father, who
had had his own anxieties on this point,

prevailed upon her to give up the engage-
ments she had made with apparent zest,
and resort to Naples and Sorrento.

To Naples, accordingly, they went, the
faithful Ralph accompanying them, at the
cost of a night-journey on his return to
Rome for the day that was to see his happiness in flower. He drove with them to
their hotel, through the interminable streets,
lined with palaces and thronged with paupers, and saw them ensconced in pleasant
quarters facing Vesuvius, whose feather of
smoke pointed to good weather. They
dined together in a vast *salle-à-manger*,
where, in a gallery, was conducted during
their repast a noisy and mirth-provoking
concert of fiddlers, mandolins, and guitars,
— the performers singing, shouting, danc-
ing, as they played. There was an hour
before his train left, in which, while the
Colonel smoked upon the balcony of their
sitting-room, Eve walked out upon one of
the quays with her cousin ; and this hour
Ralph determined to improve.

In the last day or two, trifles had shown
this astute young man that the depression
of his cousin (for whom he cherished no

grudge because, a year or two before, he
had been wild to call her wife, and she
would not hear of it) had been coincident
with the meeting in Rome with Townsend. That very morning, he had found
at his bankers', had read and put into his
pocket, a letter written by Vance on arriving at Taormina, which had thrown
upon the subject a new and surprising
light. Just how to convey his discoveries
to Evelyn, the most proud and sensitive
of creatures about her sacred feelings, he
had not yet decided.

They talked of the bay, of the mountains, of Vesuvius. Calmed and enchanted
by the hour and scene, Eve wore her gen-
tlest aspect, and Ralph felt emboldened to
begin.

"This is as it should be," he said, with
an air of generalizing. "You will go to
Sorrento and Amalfi and Capri, and your
roses will come back. I shall not forget
you, Evie dear, because I am getting what
I most want in life. You have always
been to me a thing apart, and I've told
Maud so, over and over again. By and
by, I shall bring her to the Hall, and let

her see you at your best, as its mistress.
For you are not quite the same over here,
Evie, as in Virginia air."

"Perhaps I am growing old," she said,
smiling. "But never mind me. We
shall miss you, Ralph, and it will require
the greatest heroism to do without you.
After this journey, nobody need tell me
that 'three is trumpery.' We know better, do we not?"

"Why not send for your other cousin
to take my place?" said Ralph, seeing his
opportunity. "He is at Taormina, and
would come, undoubtedly. I had a letter
from him this morning, by the way. The
most characteristic letter, — just like the
man."

No answer. Ralph felt as he were
treading a bridge of glass.

"To explain it, I should have to go
back to the evening of that meeting in
the Baths of Caracalla. He came to me
at the hotel, and after a friendly chat, just
as he was leaving, took occasion to say
some uncommonly nice things about my
relations with (as I thought) *Maud*; so I
thanked him, and gushed a little about her,

maybe,—in my circumstances, a fellow's excusable,—and off he went, I never sus- pecting that he all the time thought I was going to marry *you*."

Here Ralph was rewarded by a genuine start and a blush, but still Eve did not speak.

" A day later," Ralph went on, determined now to do or die, "something I recalled of our conversation made me realize the mistake he was under, and I wrote him a letter explaining it.   Such a time as I had to find his whereabouts! His banker had no instructions to forward anything, and I won't tell you all the ups and downs of trying to get at him.   Finally, in despair, I sent the letter, on the chance, to Taormina, and from there he answered me."

At this point, in revenge for her indifference, the diplomatist remained, in his turn, silent, until Eve, who could bear it no longer, turned upon him her beautiful young face, glowing in the evening light with an eager joy.   " And — and ? " she exclaimed, impetuously.

" He is a good sort — Townsend,"

went on Ralph, reflectively. "I've an idea, Evie, that if you and he could have managed to hit it off, you would have suited each other capitally. He would be the kind likely to settle down into a country gentleman, too; and you would never be happy in town. He has brains and a heart, in addition to his good looks and manners, and a restrained force of character that would be an excellent balance for this little impulsive lady, whose only fault is that she jumps at conclusions instead of working to them."

"You are perfectly right about that, Ralph," she said, laughing away a strong desire to cry. "I am learning wisdom, however, with rapidly advancing years. And you do only justice to my Cousin Vance, in your estimate of him. No doubt," here she swallowed a nervous catch in her voice, "if he told the truth in his letter, he congratulated you upon being allied to some one other than the young person who made his visit to Virginia last year a very hard test of patience, to say no more."

She stopped, and tried to turn away her

head. But Ralph, looking her gently in the face, read there what gave him cour- age to launch the last arrow in his quiver.

"Whatever he said, I saw through it, Evie dear. And I — I could not wait to write an answer. I telegraphed my advice to come to Naples as fast as steam can carry him."

Shortly after her conversation upon the quay with Ralph (who, returning to Rome, had been duly translated into anticipated bliss), Eve and her father took advantage of a perfect Sunday for the excursion up Mount Vesuvius.

In a landau with two horses, — a third to be annexed on the ascent, — they traversed the long street formed by the villages of San Giovanni, La Barra, Portici, and Resina, stretching from the parent city — a street suggesting in the matter of population a series of scattered ant-hills. Such a merry, dirty, shameless horde of all ages, who, abandoning the dens they called homes, had issued forth under the sun blazing even at that early hour of morning in his vault of blue, to bivouac

[*95*]

in the open highway, was never seen!
Marketing, chaffering, vending, gossiping,
cooking, eating, drinking, performing the
rites of religion and of the toilet, the
hum of their voices was like the note of
some giant insect. It was when a stranger's carriage came in sight that the air
became suddenly vocal with shrill cries
for alms; vehicles and horses were sur-
rounded, escorted by noisy beggars, whose
half-naked children offered flowers, or
turned somersaults perilously near the
wheels.

Resina passed, they could breathe more
freely. The street turmoil was succeeded
by the peace of a country road mounting
between lava walls, over which glimpses
of sea, of deep-red clover in fields, of vine-
yard or lemon grove, were finally succeeded by glorious, unobstructed views of
the mountains, bay, and city. In the region of recent overflows, they saw the
most curious spectacle, to the newcomer,
of fertile garden-strips of green, where
clung tiny houses, pink or whitewashed,
daring the mute monster overhead, while
close beside them the mountain-side was

streaked with ominous stains marking the spots where other homes had defied him just one day too long.

Higher still, in the track of the overflow of 1872, they experienced the striking effect of entering into a valley of desolation between walls of living green. Here, the lava in settling had wreathed itself into the forms of dragons couchant, of huge serpents, and other monstrous shapes that lay entwined as if asleep. Up above, arose the main cone of the crater, smooth as a heap of gun-powder, vast, majestic, cloud-circled; taking upon itself in the intense light a blooming purple tint; the smoke issuing from its summit now soon melting into space, now showing dense and threatening.

Evelyn, in whom the novelty as well as beauty of the scene had aroused fresh spirit, looked more like her old self than her fond father had seen her for many a long day. But it is fortunately not given to parents, however solicitous, to see all the workings of young minds; and the good gentleman would have been indeed surprised had he divined the mainspring of

her animation. While he was indulging
in a few mild objections to the length and
slowness of the drive, the rapacity of
wayside beggars, the heat of the sun, etc.,
such as naturally occur to the traveller
unsupported by sentimental hopes, to our
young lady the condition of motion was a
necessity, and the act of getting upward
a relief.

For the plain truth was that, since the
last talk with Ralph, Evelyn had given
rein to a thousand emotions repressed,
during the months gone by, with stern
self-chiding.

Until now, recalling the year before
when Vance had left her to an unavailing
sense of regret for her harsh judgment of
him, she had hardly realized what their
intercourse together had meant to her.
But the period of his visit was, in fact,
succeeded by one in which her salt of life
had lost its savor; and Evelyn, to her dismay, found that her affections had gone
from her keeping to this man's, acknowl-
edged to have been the suitor of her
friend.

That Katherine had refused Vance,

and straightway married another lover,
made very little difference to one of Eve's
rigid creed in these matters. To her,
love declared was love unchangeable;
with all her heart she pitied Vance for his
disappointment, and blamed herself for
having repeatedly wounded him without
reason. By means of this mode of argument, she had naturally succeeded in rais-
ing Townsend to the pedestal of a mar-
tyred hero, which, it may be conceived by
those of colder judgment, did not lessen
his importance in the girl's imagination.

As the months had gone on, and she
had had nothing from him save packages
of books and prints sent according to promise, as to a polite entertainer who is thus
agreeably disposed of by the beneficiary
of hospitality extended, her feelings had
taken on the complexion of hopeless regret
for an irrevocable past. What Eve had
henceforth to do, according to her own
strict ordinance, was to live down the impulse that made her give her heart unasked.
The stress of these emotions had, in spite
of her brave efforts, so worked upon her
health that the Colonel, as fond of home

as a limpet of his rock, determined to try
for her the change of air and experience,
resulting as we have seen.

And now, on this dazzling day, a " bridal of earth and sky " in one of the loveliest spots upon earth, she kept saying to herself, " By to-morrow — to-morrow, at latest — he will be with me ! And then — and then — and *then* — ! "

The carriage halted at a little wayside booth for the sale of wines and fruit. A dark-skinned woman, bearing a tray of glasses, with flasks of the delusive *Lachrymae Christi* (made from the grapes ripened upon these slopes) came forward to greet them. On Evelyn's side, a hawker, with shells and strings of coral, and coins alleged to have been found imbedded in the lava near at hand, importuned her. But, rejecting the others, she beckoned to a pretty, bare-legged boy carrying oranges garnished in their own glossy, dark-green leaves; and so busy was she in selecting the best of his refreshing fruit, she hardly observed that another claimant for her attention had appeared close beside the wheel.

"Please go away, my good man," she said at last, laughingly, without giving him a glance. "Indeed, I want nothing you can supply."

"That is a harsh assertion," Vance said, in a low tone meant for her ear, and then proceeded to greet both his cousins outspokenly.

He had reached Naples early that morning; had ascertained at their hotel that they were engaged to start for Vesuvius at a given hour; fearing collision with a party of strangers, had set out alone to walk up the mountain and take his chance of intercepting them; and had waited here for the purpose.

"After you had been journeying all night?" said the Colonel, with unfeigned surprise. "Why, my dear fellow, in your place I should have —"

Just then he intercepted, passing between Evelyn and Vance, a look that startled him. That his sentence remained unfinished nobody observed. The Colonel drew back into his corner, as if he had been shot.

If she had divined her father's feeling,

Eve could not have pitied any one who was gaining Vance. And Vance, at that moment, believed all the world to be as happy as himself!

To a love-affair so obvious, the ending naturally to be expected is of the old-fashioned and inevitable sort. In the beautiful Indian summer of the following autumn in Virginia, these two people were duly married at the Hall. From far and wide came relatives to wish them joy; it was like the gathering of a Scotch clan at the summons of the pipes. Prominent among the revellers at the dance following the nuptial ceremony was Cousin Josey, who, in a pair of antiquated leather pumps with buckles, led down the middle of a reel with his cherished " Lady-love." To please the old boy, Evelyn had worn the little string of pearls bought by him, years before, for a bride who was never to be. And so everybody was content, and one of the cousins said it was "exactly like a weddin' befo' the wah."

Out of Season

Chapter I

"NO; no house-parties till the mid- Out of
dle of July. Dear knows, what Season
with a string of big dinners, my two little
dances, and those tiresome Thursdays in
January and February when everybody
came, I have done all that could be expected by society from paupers like ourselves," said Mrs. Henry Gervase, settling
herself in a wicker chair, on the veranda
of her country home, and looking approvingly at her water-view.

"Paupers!" said a lady from a neigh-
boring cottage, who had dropped in to call.
Mrs. Gervase's friends rarely liked to com-
mit themselves to positive comment upon
her statements until certain which way the
cat was meant to jump. Mrs. Luther
Prettyman, the wife of the dry-goods mag-
nate, whose good fortune it was to own
the land adjoining the Gervase property at
Sheepshead Point, — a recently famous resort for summer visitors on our far eastern

coast, — now contented herself with a little deprecatory giggle that might mean anything, and waited for Mrs. Gervase to go on.

"Oh, well! everything is comparative; and on the scale by which people measure things in New York, to-day, we are simply grovelling in poverty. John," — to her gardener, — "you have got that row of myosotis entirely out of line; and, remember, nothing but salvia behind the heliotropes. I like a blaze of scarlet and purple against a blue sea-line like this. Heavens! what a perfect afternoon! The atmosphere has been clarified, and those birches in the ravine 'twinkle with a million lights.' My dear woman, I make no apologies. Any one who wants me at this season of the year must take me as I am. After eight months of bricks and mortar, dirty streets, and stupid drives in the Park, I am fairly maudlin over Nature when I get her back in June.

"I went to a concert where Paderewski played a night or two before he left America; and I give you my word that while the music was going on I put up my

fan and plainly heard the babble of this
little brook of mine, and the lap of the
waves over the rocks at high tide, with,
now and then, the notes of the song-
sparrow that comes back every year and
perches on my Norway pine. Somebody
said of me afterwards, at supper, that I
had been having a little nap. They may
say anything of me, I believe, and some
idiot will be found to credit it. But please
don't accept the newspaper report that I
am to have Mr. and Mrs. This, or Mr.
That and Mrs. T' other, stopping with me
at Stoneacres during June. I am much
too busy with my granger-work, and my
husband too industrious doing nothing, to
play host and hostess now."

"I did not know; I only thought —"
ventured Mrs. Prettyman. "You see,
everything is so dull here, socially, till
August. And when one has a guest coming who is accustomed to a great deal of
fashionable gaiety, — a young lady, a dis-
tinguished belle, — one naturally grasps at
the idea of such pleasant house-parties as
yours are known to be, dear Mrs. Gervase."

"We shall be dull as ditch-water," answered relentless Mrs. Gervase, turning
around to survey the struggle of a fat-
breasted robin to extract from the turf a
worm that continued to emerge in apparently unending length. "And if you *will*
have a girl out of season, why, put her on
bread and milk and beauty-sleep, give her
plenty of trashy novels and a horse to ride,
and she'll do well enough."

"But — perhaps I am wrong — surely
Mr. Gervase told Mr. Prettyman, when
they were smoking on our veranda last
Sunday, that you are expecting your
nephew, Mr. Alan Grove."

"That's just like Mr. Gervase, — a perfect sieve for secrets," quoth Mrs. Gervase, contemptuously; "when I particularly
requested him to mention Alan's visit to
nobody. The poor boy is completely used
up with work, and has engaged to get a
paper ready to read before some scientific
congress next month, and finds himself
unable to write a line of it in town. Here,
I have promised him, he may have absolute quiet — not be called on to play civility or squire-of-dames for any one; and, I

may as well warn you *now*, he's not to be
expected to do a *hand's turn* of entertainment for your girl.   Besides, I happen to
know that he can't abide ' society ' young
women.   He is plunged up to the neck in
electricity, is poor, ambitious, clever, on
the way to sure success ; and I 'm going
to back him all I can, not put stumbling-
blocks in his path."

"How plunged up to his neck in electricity ? " asked puzzled Mrs. Prettyman.

"Electric law, my good soul ; did you
think it a new kind of capital punishment ?
The lucrative law of the future, I 've heard
wise men say.   Simpkins ! " hailing, with
irresistible command, a butcher's cart that
seemed possessed of a strong desire to
drive away in a hurry from a side entrance
to the house. "*Simpkins !* Oh ! there you
are ; I meant to leave orders with the cook
not to let you get away again to-day without a word from me.   I noticed, on the
book, that you had the effrontery to charge
sixty cents a pound for spring chickens
here in June.   Now, don't tell me ! The
way all you natives do ; you have a short
season, and must make the most of it.

This is not your season, or my season, either. Wait till August before you put on the screws. And your sweetbreads, eighty cents a pair, when *you know* that when Mr. Gervase and I first came here to live, you were *throwing sweetbreads away*, till we taught you the use of them! Now, mind, I shall get tired of sending friends to you to be fleeced in August, if this is what you do to me in June."

"I must be running off," said Mrs. Prettyman, arising from her spot of shade and luxurious comfort in the deep veranda filled, though not encumbered, with picturesque belongings, with stands and pots of blooming plants in every nook. "I 'll declare, nobody's flowers do as well as yours. And the wages we pay our head gardener! It makes me really envious."

This, be it known, was a clever stroke on the part of neighbor Prettyman. Secretly resentful of the tepid interest in the personality of her expected guest, — who, in the eyes of the house of Prettyman, was an event, — she yet did not dare attempt to bring the greater lady to yield sympathy upon the spot. Mrs. Gervase's weakest

side was for her flowers. She possessed
the magic touch that alone nurtures them
to perfection, and with it the proud love
of a parent for children that grow inclined
according to her will.

"Hum! We do pretty well, considering
this house is built on the ragged edge of
nothing over the sea, and is swept by all
the winds of heaven, in turn, and some-
times all together. And, in a climate
where one goes to bed in the Tropics and
wakes up at the North Pole, what would
you have? John, there, though I'll not
set him up by telling him so, has learned
all I know about flowers, and picks up
new ideas every day. By August, now,
these beds and stands will be worth looking at. What did you say is the name of
the young person who's coming to stop
with you? If you've nothing better, suppose you and she and Mr. Prettyman come
over to dinner Saturday. Alan has promised me not to work at night, and by that
time my plants will all be in the ground
and my mind at rest."

"Thank you so much," said the lesser
luminary. "It is always a treat to dine

with you *en famille;* and it is — did n't I
mention her ? — Gladys Eliot who is coming to us to-morrow."

"Gladys Eliot ! Why, she 's gone with
her people to London for two months. I
saw her name in the *Teutonic's* list last
Thursday. Those Eliots would never in
the world let slip another chance for her
to make the great match they 've set out
to get."

"Nevertheless," said Mrs. Prettyman,
with some show of spirit, "Mrs. Eliot,
who is my old school-friend, wrote me, the
day before they sailed, that Gladys had
taken it into her head to stay behind, and
begged me to keep her till her aunt can
come up from Baltimore in July and take
the girl in charge."

"Three weeks of Gladys Eliot !" remarked Mrs. Gervase. "My poor woman,
I pity you. By the end of the month
there will be no health in you. A professional beauty, who has run the gauntlet
of four or five years of incessant praises,
has been advertised like 'Pear's Soap,' in
England and America, and has failed to
make her *coup !* I remember what Alan

Grove said about her no longer ago than
Christmas of last year: 'I have n't the
advantage of Miss Eliot's acquaintance,
but her and her kind I hold in abhorrence,
— denationalized Americans; hangers-on
of older civilizations that make a puppet-
show of them; spoiled for home, with
no rightful place abroad; restless, craving
what no healthy-minded husband of their
own kind can give them.' Bless me —
and *those two* are going to *meet here !*"

"I think Mr. Alan Grove need not
concern himself," said Mrs. Prettyman,
driven to bay. "Mrs. Eliot mentioned in
her letter that Gladys — it is no secret,
evidently — is nearly, if not quite, engaged to marry some one the family feels
is *in all respects* all they could have hoped
for her."

"Then it must be either that Colonel
Larkyns, the very rude man with large
feet, who walked all over my velvet gown
at the Egertons', last winter, — came over
with Lord Glenmore, whom the Eliots
tried for and could n't get, — or else Mc-
Laughlin, the Irishman who made such a
lot of money in Montana. The two men

[*113*]

were running evenly, 't was said.   Let me
think — did n't I see her at Claremont on
McLaughlin's coach, last month ?   Pray,
my dear, are we to congratulate you on
having Mr. McLaughlin, also, as a member of your household, before long ? "

"Oh dear, dear ! " continued the plain-
spoken lady to herself, when poor Mrs.
Prettyman, fairly routed, had retired without honors from the field.   " Why is
nature so heavenly kind to us in American
places of resort, and ' only man is vile ' ?
Why does this struggle for place, this
pride of vogue, these types of our worst
social element — I hate that word ' social,'
it sounds vulgar ; but what else expresses
this for me ? — follow one into this earthly
Paradise ?   Here I have got myself into
a pretty kettle of fish with Alan Grove.
He will be bored to death and his visit
broken up, for we can't rid ourselves
of people who sit in our pocket, like
the Prettymans in summer ; and he will
be running upon this Eliot creature per-
petually.   If Henry would help me, we
might — but he is so abominably friendly
and cordial with country neighbors, there 's

no hope from him.   Besides, if a girl is *Out of*
pretty, it makes no earthly difference to *Season*
my good man whether she is a fiend of
calculation and cold-heartedness.   I declare, I've no patience with Henry, any-
how."

So saying, Mrs. Gervase went out to
drive with the offender in question, behind
a pair of sleek cobs, in a little buckboard
of tawny wood with russet leather cushions and harness, — his latest present, —
and soon, in cheerful companionship, forgot all sorrows amid such views of land
and water as Sheepshead Point people
think only Sheepshead Point can offer.

Chapter II

TO reach Sheepshead Point, a boat steams daily, and several times a day, from a station on the line of a great railway skirting the eastern Atlantic coast. Issuing from a drawing-room car there, a young woman, dressed in a tight-fitting skirt and jacket of sailor blue, with a loose shirt of red silk belted around a taper waist, her small head with its sailor-hat half shrouded from view in a blue tissue veil, walked lightly ahead of Mr. Alan Grove and, attended by an elderly maid, went far forward to stand in the bows of the boat.

Grove, struck by the grace and distinction of her carriage, looked again, and then was conscious of an actual fierce jump of the heart.

"Can there be two of them?" he asked of his inner man. "Doctors tell you if you keep your body in good order, and your mind healthily at work, you will never see a ghost — and yet — that's the

double of the woman who sailed away *Out of*
from me last Thursday; who's haunted *Season*
me during the six madly misspent weeks
since I had the misfortune to be told off
to take her in to dinner. Oh! no, it is n't.
Yes, it is — by Jove, it *is* Gladys Eliot."

He was never so astonished. Believing her to be at that moment on the ocean, nearing British shores, Grove was fairly staggered when Miss Eliot, turning, espied him and, by a graciously easy nod, summoned him to her side. Considering the manner of their parting a few weeks back, he wondered at himself for the immediate abjectness of his obedience.

It was a favorite phrase of Gladys Eliot's admirers to describe her as having a " Duchess of Leinster head and throat." Nature had certainly bestowed upon this daughter of nobody in particular in the Western Hemisphere a pose of a proud little head upon broad, sloping shoulders, as fine as that much-photographed great lady's. She had, in addition, a pair of innocent, Irish-blue eyes and a guileless smile; a voice, in speaking, that was sweet and low; and the best or worst manners in

[*117*]

" Mr. Grove! How perfectly extraordinary that you should be here," she
exclaimed, giving him the tips of her
well-gloved fingers, while the maid and
dressing-bag withdrew discreetly into the
background.

" Did you expect me to remain forever
on the steps of the Claremont tea-house,
like a monument of a city father, to adorn
the suburbs of New York ? "

" You are so quick-tempered, so unreasonable! How should I know you were
going to take such dire offence? But
please — I can't quarrel away off here,
or even justify myself. If you are going
to remain furious with me, at least gratify
my curiosity first, and tell me how you
came on this boat, and where you are
going. Then, if you are so inclined, you
may retire into your shell and sulk."

A soft light was shining in her eye.
Her voice was pleading; her face, most
beautiful. Grove, promising himself, in
street vernacular, to " go off and kick himself " directly afterwards, took his place

at her elbow and gazed down hungrily
upon her artless, changeful countenance.

" Rather tell me why you are not about
to plant your triumphant banner on British shores once more. I read your name
in the list of those sailing. The newspapers have given all of your summer plans
in detail, all the country-houses that are to
receive you, all the aristocrats that are to
send invitations to dinner, to meet your
ship at Queenstown."

She colored slightly. " As usual, you
are making fun of me. What would be
the use, since you won't believe me, of
telling you my actual reason for backing
out of this English visit, and letting my
mother and sister go without me ? No, I
shan't flatter you by showing my real self."

" I have seen enough of your real self,
thank you. I believe I prefer the unreal,
the imaginary woman I suffered myself to
fancy you to be for a brief space after our
acquaintance began."

" Now you are rude," she began, her
voice faltering ever so little, but enough
to shake his equilibrium. He made a
movement towards her; and she looked

[*119*]

him in the face, trying to keep down the
tingle of satisfaction in her veins. For
Gladys's experience of men had taught
her to recognize in a certain phase of in-
civility the existence of passion unsubdued.
It is only indifference in his sex that can
maintain an armor of polite self-control
towards hers.

Grove caught the transient gleam in her
eye, and read it aright. Immediately he
was on the defensive, and his manner
froze.

" I believe you know my aunt, Mrs.
Gervase, in town," he said. " I think I
saw you at one of her dances, in January."

" Mrs. Gervase is the dearest thing,"
interrupted Miss Eliot, conscious of blankness in her tone.

" She may be, but it would be a brave
person who would tell her so. She is a
delightful, but autocratic, personage ; and
one of the treats of the year for me is to
get away to her and my uncle for a holiday, when they have no one else. This
is one of those rare occasions. The cottage people who have come down to
Sheepshead have a tacit agreement to keep

to themselves, just now. They are supposed to be getting their houses to rights,
and making gardens, and what not. Mrs.
Gervase says they are really wearing out
the past season's gloves, and putting tonics
on their hair, and trying new cures and
doses, for which there was no time before
leaving town. The days will pass in doing as we please, and in the evening we
shall dine well (for the Gervases have a
corker of a cook), after which my aunt
and uncle and I will take each a book and
a lamp into some nook of the library, and
read till bedtime. You can't imagine a
life more to my taste."

"Prohibitory to outsiders, at least," said
Gladys. "This is, as I suppose you mean
it to be, awfully alarming to me; for I
have n't told you that I am for three weeks
to be Mrs. Gervase's nearest neighbor. I
am going to visit an old friend of my mother's, — Mrs. Luther Prettyman."

Grove experienced a sensation of dismay. The Prettymans! Château Calicot, as he had dubbed their new florid
"villa," built on the shore in objectionable
proximity to his uncle's house, some three

years back! He remembered the vines planted, the shrubs set out, the rattan screens hung, the final adjustment of chairs by Mrs. Gervase, in the attempt to shut out every glimpse of the Prettyman belongings from their place of daily rendezvous on the veranda at Stoneacres; his uncle's sly amusement when the cupola of the Prettyman stables, and the roof of a detestable little sugar-temple tea-house were projected on their line of vision, spite of all. Mrs. Gervase could not forgive herself for not having secured that point of land when land was so ridiculously cheap. On an average of once a day, she reminded her husband that she had begged him to do so, and he had put it off until too late.

Mrs. Prettyman, unvisited by Mrs. Gervase for many months after the red-brown gables of her costly dwelling rose into prominence at Sheepshead Point, had gradually found her way into quasi-intimacy at Stoneacres. Mrs. Gervase, protesting that her neighbor was commonplace, vacuous, a being from whom one could derive nothing more profitable than the address of a place in town to have one's lace lamp-

shades made a dollar cheaper than elsewhere, allowed herself, in time, to take a
mild but perceptible interest in Prettyman
affairs. Through force of habit, she had
grown accustomed to survey the Prettyman lodge-gates, in driving, without re-
marking upon " the absurdity of gilded
finials to iron railings, at a rough, seaside
place like this." Nay, the noses of the
Gervase cobs were now not infrequently
turned in through these gilded railings.
Mr. and Mrs. Gervase dined periodically
with the Prettymans. The Prettymans
repaired more frequently to Stoneacres.
Mrs. Prettyman made capital, in town, of
her friendship with " dear Mrs. Gervase."
This, Grove, like the rest of the world,
had come gradually to know and accept.
But it grated on him to hear that the
woman who, so far, had furnished his life
its chief feminine influence should be associated in this way with the mistress of
Château Calicot. It belittled his one passion — now put away as dead, but still his
own. This, indeed, set the crowning
touch upon his misfortune of meeting her
again.

Chapter III

"MY dear boy, you might have knocked me down with a feather," said Mrs. Gervase, upon capturing her nephew at the wharf and driving away with him. "Tell me at once what you mean by knowing Gladys Eliot, and arriving with her in that intimate sort of way, just as I had, with infinite trouble, succeeded in bluffing the Prettymans with a mere dinner on Saturday! Now you will be *having* to call. *You*, of all people, hitting it off with Gladys Eliot!"

"Give yourself no concern," put in Mr. Gervase, who was driving, looking back over his shoulder with a beaming smile; "I offer to throw myself into the breach. A woman as beautiful, as tall, as placid, as Miss Eliot commands the best homage of my heart. I forewarn you that I am going desperately into this affair. Such luck never came my way before."

[*124*]

"Stop at the confectioner's for the macaroons, Henry," said his wife, ignoring transports. "Alan, you are looking wretched. When I think of those ruddy, brown cheeks, and the look of vigor you brought out of your college athletics a few years back, I'm inclined to renounce mind and go in for muscle exclusively. Oh, that wretched grind of life in New York that crushes the youth and spirit out of you poor boys that have to toil for a living! Surely, it is n't *only* law that's worked such havoc in those pale, thin cheeks—"

"My dear Agatha, your sympathy would put a well man in his bed," said Mr. Gervase, whose keen eyes took in more of the actual situation than did his wife's.

"Oh well!—stop here, please; no, I won't get down, Jonas sees me; he will be out directly, with the parcel — you must see, Henry, that Alan has changed, even since—"

"Alan, let me tell you of a bill our friend Jonas, here, who is a bit of a horse-jockey, as well as local confectioner and pastry-cook, sent in recently to your aunt. He had been selling her a mate to her chestnut, and the account ran this way :

" 'MRS. H. GERVASE TO I. JONAS, DR.

1 lb. lady-fingers	. .	$ 0.30
One horse	. . .	250.00
½ lb. cream peppermints	.	0.20

Total, $250.50 ' "

Grove was glad to cover his various discomforts with a laugh. But he did not find it easy to elude the vigilance of Mrs. Gervase, who bided her time until an opportunity presented itself for an uninterrupted talk with him.

"Stretch yourself out on that bamboo couch, and let me put the pillows in," she said, when they two adjourned to the veranda, in the twilight after dinner. "It is such fun to have a boy to cosset once more, with my own lads at college, and three weeks to wait before I can get Tom and Louis back from New London after the boat-race."

"You have such an inspired faculty for making men comfortable," Grove

remarked, from the depths of his *bien-*
être.

"Custom, I suppose. An only daughter, with a father and three brothers to wait upon till I married, and a husband and two sons to impose on me since. I should not know how to handle girls. I like them, of course, — find them all very well in their way, — but they bother me. Perhaps it is that there are no old-fashioned girls any more — no young ones, certainly. They come into the world like Minerva from Jove's brain. They are so learned, or clever, or worldly-wise, read everything, see everything, hear everything discussed, have no illusions — but, there, I can't explain my preference. Men are captious, obstinate, whimsical, by turns; disappoint one continually in little things — but in the main they are so broad and big; scatter nonsense into thin air; are so loyal and unswerving to their beliefs; know where they stand, and, having made up their minds to action, do not change."

"In short," remarked Grove, "you are

Out of like the little servant-maid in Cranford,
Season when they told her to hand the potatoes
to the ladies first. 'I'll do as you bid me,
ma'am, but I like the lads best.' My
dearest auntie, there must be guardian an-
gels specially appointed to look after our
sex, and you are one of them. This is
the age and America is the field for the
unchecked efflorescence of young woman-
kind. But when the conversation takes
on this complexion, I feel it to be unfair
not to allow the defendant the assistance
of counsel; though, even if Uncle Henry
were here, I am sure we should both be
demolished speedily."

"Never mind Henry," said that gentleman's representative. "He has got a new
letter from a man in London whom he
keeps for the purpose of making him mis-
erable with catalogues of sales of books
and papers he can't afford to buy. But
he potters over them, and marks the lists,
and writes back to the man in London,
and, as you know, we do manage to become possessed of much more dear an-
tiquity than the house will hold or our in-
come warrant. This time, he is buried

alive for an hour to come, for it is about a sale of Sir Philip Francis's letters and manuscripts at Sotheby's very soon."

"I don't believe the real 'Junius' announcing himself would get me out of this bamboo chair and away from this deepening of eventide upon the sea and islands, the afterglow of sunset melting into moonlight, the soft caressing of the salt air blending with those hidden heliotropes of yours! Now, dear lady, let's go back to the concrete. I knew, the moment your eagle eye fell on me this afternoon, you would find out all that in me is. For so many years I've been telling you my scrapes, I may as well out with the latest and biggest of them. Two months ago, I took Gladys Eliot in to dinner at the Sargents'. I kept it from you in town, for which you'll say I am properly punished. I fell in love with her, like a schoolboy with green apples, heeding not the danger of unwholesomeness. After that, I met her when and wherever I could push my way to her. I thought of her, sleeping and waking; received from her looks and tones and words that would, as

" My poor child, how wretched!" said Mrs. Gervase, promptly.

" So it proved. Last but not least of the comedy, — I skip the details, — I was deluded into buttoning myself up in a fluffy, long-tailed, iron-gray coat that I got in London last spring and had not had time to wear, put on a bunch of white carnations, and drove out to one of those inane Claremont teas in my friend Pierre Sargent's trap, because, forsooth, *she* asked me. For an hour I suffered martyrdom in that little greenhouse sort of a veranda, with people herded together gossiping, and not setting their feet upon the lawn over the river that they came out to see. Women talked drivel to me, waiters slopped tea over me, and we walked on slices of buttered bread. Then *she* came — on the box-seat of that brute Mc-Laughlin's drag, having eyes for him only, so that every one talked of it!"

" I remember — and I could not imagine what brought you there. Yes, I sat down on a little cake and completely

ruined my new porcelain-blue *crépon* —
those waiters were very careless. Jolly
faded it trying to take out the spot, and
Mathilde had the greatest trouble to match
the stuff. Alan, that man McLaughlin
ought to be drummed out of polite society. The girl who would receive his at-
tentions, let herself be talked of as likely
to be his wife, cannot at heart be nice.
When your dear mother and I were girls,
we would not have *looked* at a big, vulgar
creature like that, simply because he drove
four-in-hand and was known to be rich.
He would never have been asked to your
grandfather's table. The materialism of
this age takes, to me, no form more objectionable than the frank acceptance of such
as he by women, old and young."

" Exactly," said Grove, grimly. " And
when I met her at his side, she turned
away from him one moment with a banal
jest for me, and then quickly recaptured
him, as if fearful he would escape. That,
even my infatuation would not suffer. I
turned on my heel, and, until I met her
by chance on the boat to-day, have never
seen her since."

"What can have been her reason for not going abroad?" said Mrs. Gervase, eagerly — a trifle suspiciously.

Grove was silent. In his ear sounded a dulcet voice, murmuring as the boat neared shore: "Perhaps, when you have consented to feel better friends with me, you will come and let me tell you *why I stayed.*"

"You know, of course, that everybody says she is engaged? Her mother has hinted it to Mrs. Prettyman. If it be to this McLaughlin, then God knows you are well rid of her. If that be a blind, Alan dear, — you know it was always my way with you boys to scold about little things and let great ones pass, — I shan't add a word to your self-reproach; but I'll warn you — oh! I won't have the sin on my soul of letting you go unwarned. That woman, no matter whether she thinks she loves you or not, would make your misery. The parents of to-day don't trouble themselves to train up wives for the rank and file of our honest gentlemen. They create fine ladies, and look about for some one to take the expense of them off their hands. It is common talk that the Eliots have been strained to their utmost means to carry their girls from place to place, with the expectation of making rich marriages. The beauty and success of this one has apparently blinded those poor people to the consequences of their folly. The girl has been brought up to fancy herself of superior clay, — her habits are luxurious, her wants extravagant.

" More than all, for five years she has been fed on the flatteries of society. Personal praise is indispensable to her. She has lived and consorted with the most lavish entertainers of the most reckless society in our republic. Even supposing that you won her beauty and graces for your own, what on earth could you expect to offer her in exchange for what she would give up ? My poor, dear lad, I 'm talking platitudes, you think ; but you and Tom and Louis shall not be allowed to wreck your futures upon such as Gladys Eliot, while I have breath to speak. I 'm afraid I think all marriages a mistake for young men. I know they are, as we measure and value things, in what we call ' fashionable life.'

Go out of it, by all means, if you can. To take *her* out of it you would find to be quite another matter. And now, after this long homily, I've one question to put. Answer it, if you like — if you think I've the right to ask it. After seeing her again to-day, do you feel there is danger in her proximity?"

"You have certainly torn sentiment to shreds," said Alan, getting up from amid his cushions and beginning to stride up and down the long veranda. Mrs. Gervase watched him without further speech. That he did not again allude to the subject sent her to bed with keen anxiety and a renewed regret that Mr. Gervase had not taken her advice about buying that point of land before it fell into the hands of the Prettymans.

For the two or three days following his arrival at Stoneacres, Grove made no attempt to see his neighbor's guest. Once, indeed, they encountered her on horseback, while driving together in a family party in the buckboard, behind the cobs. Mr. Gervase, who, in his later enthusiasm about the Junius correspondence, had forgotten

his charmer, asked who was that stunning, Out of
pretty girl, and, on being rallied by his wife, Season
declared his poor sight was at fault, and
that he meant to call on the Prettymans
that very day; but Saturday brought with
it the appointed dinner, without other over-
ture from Stoneacres than cards left by
Mrs. Gervase when the ladies were from
home.

Grove was hardly surprised when, on
descending to the drawing-room in evening
clothes, he found only that very colorless
pair of Prettymans. Miss Eliot, it was
alleged, was suffering from too long a ride
in the hot sun of the afternoon to make
the effort to come out. He saw in the
countenance of his aunt a look of relief,
which she at once proceeded to mask by
unusual suavity to mankind in general, her
flattered guests in particular.

" The worst is over; I am safe," Grove
decided. " But I like her all the better
for that womanly holding back. Now, to
live down my folly as best I can."

He threw himself into hard work, and
the days passed healthily. Mrs. Gervase
had begun to relax her vigilance, to breathe

almost free of care, when, upon one of his morning rides, ahead of him in a forest glade, he espied Gladys Eliot, in the saddle, attended by one of the Prettyman boys, a youngster of thirteen, mounted on a polo pony in process of " showing off " his and his master's accomplishments.

At the sound behind them, both Gladys and the boy turned to look ; and Grove saw that he could not retreat without a decided lack of dignity. He therefore rode by them, receiving from Miss Eliot a faint and chilly nod; from the boy,—an acquaintance of last year, —a more cordial salutation.

" I say, Mr. Grove, *can't* Punch take that fallen tree ? " cried out the lad, in shrill treble. " *She* says it's dangerous, because the bank is caved. Hold on one minute, and I'll show you he can clear it, bank and all."

Punch, proving nothing loth, jumped the obstacles in question gallantly, but on the far side slipped on something, and spilled his rider among a bed of tall bracken, in which the boy lay, lost to sight. Both Grove and Gladys were in a minute at his

[*136*]

side, shocked at finding him white and senseless.

"It was not the fall," she said, rapidly. "He has heart-trouble, and his mother is always anxious about a sudden shock for him. He will outgrow it probably, the doctors say. Here, you hold him in your arms, while I get water from that brook. I know what to do, and he will soon come to himself."

Grove found himself silently obeying her behests. He was struck by her prompt presence of mind, her deftness, and good sense. "What an admirable trained nurse is lost to the world in her!" he thought, and, when all was done, and the boy gave token of returning life, sat still, content to crush down moss and ferns, awkwardly holding his burden, while Gladys knelt so close that her breath in speaking fanned his cheek.

"It was n't Punch's fault. I 've got a big bee buzzing in my head," were the welcome words they at last heard from the sufferer.

"Yes, I know, Jim dear, but don't talk now till the big bee flies away," and

the boy, closing his eyes, appeared to
sleep.

"Lay his head on my lap, and then, if
you don't mind riding back and ordering
some sort of a trap, without letting his
mother know —"

"I can't leave you here. It is too far
from home, and the country hereabouts is
quite bare of dwellings. Nor would I
like you to ride so far alone. There;
let him sleep, and we will watch him till
he wakes. No doctor could have treated
him more cleverly than you."

"It's the result of a 'First Aid to the
Injured' class I went to once, perhaps.
But I always had a knack with ill people,"
she said, dropping the deep fringes of her
eyes upon damask cheeks.

That evening, Grove could do no less
than call to inquire after Master Jim,
who, not much the worse for his attack,
kept his adoring mother in durance at his
bedside, while Grove sat watching the opal
flushes die out of a western sky, in company with Gladys. Quite another Gladys

was this, in all save beauty and her dulcet voice, from his enslaver of town life.

And now, to Mrs. Gervase's ill-concealed dismay, visits, meetings, rides, boating, began and continued daily. Grove was teaching Miss Eliot chess, he said, and the other things were what they call upon the stage "incidental divertisements."

A fortnight of glorious weather had passed thus, when, on the eve of Grove's return to town and work, he asked Gladys to go out in a boat with him to watch the sunset on the water.

"Now you have told me there is no reason I may not speak, I can wait no longer for an answer," he said, as, resting on his oars, he scanned her face eagerly. "When a man tears his heart out and throws it at a woman's feet, surely he offers something. But that, you know, is my all. If you can consent to share the kind of life mine has got to be for the next five or six years, I think I see daylight beyond. By that time, your first youth will be gone, you will be forgotten by the

people who court you now, you will be a
nobody in their esteem. To me, you will
always be the one woman of the world.
You will have the full love of my heart;
and you shall see what that means, when
a true man pours it upon you unrestrained.
I don't pretend to be worth it, Heaven
knows. But I do say you have never before been loved by a man like me, and you
know it and feel it thoroughly. It's for
you to take or leave me, accepting consequences."

" What a stand-and-deliver kind of love-
making!" Gladys tried to say; but she
was deeply stirred. Remaining silent, her
eyes filled with tears; her head drooped
towards her breast.

" Gladys!" cried he, exultingly.

" Don't you see, now, the real reason
why I could not go abroad?" she said,
smiling on him brightly, and lifting, at the
same moment, her ungloved left hand to
put back a loose lock of hair that the wind
had blown across her cheek. Grove, gazing at her with his whole soul in his eyes,
became aware of a ring upon the fourth
finger, — a ring of such conspicuous bril-

liancy and choice gems as to convey *Out of*
but one meaning, — and his expression *Season*
changed.

"Oh! I hate it! I shall give it back!"
she exclaimed, a burning blush settling
upon her face. "I did not mean — it was
an accident. I hate it, I tell you! Why
do you look at me like that?"

She tore the ring from her hand, and
impetuously put it out of sight. Presently,
as Grove, in mechanical fashion, resumed
his rowing without a word, she cried out,
passionately:

"Why do you not ask me to explain all
the — circumstances of my life since I
saw you last? Why can't you understand
that a girl situated as I am has temptations
that at times seem to her irresistible?
Need I mortify myself by telling you that
I am *driven* — driven till I feel as if I
would do anything to get rest from eternal
lectures about what a rich marriage has
got to do for me — and for others? Yes,
you are right in saying that a man like
you never before asked me to marry him.
Because I feel that — because — because — Oh! you are cruel not to speak

[*141*]

It was impossible, facing the rigid cold-
ness of his face, to go on. She sat in
wretched silence till they reached shore,
and he gave her his chilly hand to help
her upon the float. Then the touch of
her fingers sent a tremor of relenting into
his veins.

"Oh, if I could! If I could! But he
too — that other one — believed. Tell
me; he does not still believe in you?"

"I hate him," she said, doggedly. She
shivered a little, as the quickened breeze
of evening struck her thinly-clad form.

Grove, clasping her hand, gazed into
her eyes with a desperate resolve to read
her heart.

"Let me go — it is no use," she said,
turning away from him.

And, with a sigh deep as Fate, he loos-
ened his hold of her — forever.

[*142*]

On Frenchman's Bay

.

Chapter I

FROM Maxwell Pollock, Esq., No. — Fifth Avenue, New York, to Stephen Cranbrooke, Esq., ———— Club, New York.

" May 30, 189–.

" My dear Cranbrooke :

" You will wonder why I follow up our conversation of last evening with a letter; why, instead of speaking, I should write what is left to be said between us two.

" But after a sleepless night, of which my little wife suspects nothing, I am impelled to confide in you — my oldest friend, *her* friend, although you and she have not yet grown to the comprehension of each other I hoped for when she married me three years ago — a secret that has begun to weigh heavy upon my soul.

" I do not need to remind you that, since our college days, you have known me subject to fits of moodiness and depression upon which you have often rallied me.

How many times you have said that a fellow to whom Fate had given health,
strength, opportunity, and fortune — and
recently the treasure of a lovely and loving wife — has no business to admit the
word 'depression' into his vocabulary!

"This is true. I acknowledge it, as I
have a thousand times before. I am a
fool, a coward, to shrink from what is before me. But I was still more of a fool
and a coward when I married her. For
her sake, the prospect of my death before
this summer wanes impels me to own to
you my certainty that my end is close at
hand.

"In every generation of our family
since the old fellow who came over from
England and founded us on Massachusetts
soil, the oldest son has been snatched out
of life upon the threshold of his thirtieth
year. I carried into college with me an
indelible impression of the sudden and dis-
tressing death of my father, at that period
of his prosperous career, and of the wild
cry of my widowed mother when she
clasped me to her breast, and prayed
Heaven might avert the doom from me.

"Everything that philosophy, science, *On* common sense, could bring to the task of *French-* arguing me out of a belief in the trans- *man's* mission of this sentence of a higher power *Bay* to me, has been tried. I have studied, travelled, lived, enjoyed myself in a rational way; have loved and won the one woman upon earth for me, have revelled in her wifely tenderness.

"I have tried to do my duty as a man and a citizen. In all other respects, I believe myself to be entirely rational, cool-headed, unemotional; but I have never been able to down that spectre. He is present at every feast; and, although in perfectly good health, I resolved yesterday to put the question to a practical test. I called at the office of an eminent specialist, whom I had never met, although doubtless he knew my name, as I knew his.

"Joining the throng of waiting folk in Dr. ——'s outer office, I turned over the leaves of the last number of *Punch*, with what grim enjoyment of its *menu* of jocularity you may conceive. When my turn came, I asked for a complete physical examination. But the doctor got no farther

[*147*]

than my heart before I was conscious of awakening interest on his part. When the whole business was over, he told me frankly that in what he was pleased to call 'a magnificent physique,' there was but one blemish, — a spot upon the ripe side of a peach, — a certain condition of the heart that 'might or might not' give serious trouble in the future.

"' Might or might not'! How I envied the smooth-spoken man of science his ability to say these words so glibly! While I took his medical advice, — that, between us, was not worth a straw, and he knew it, and I knew it, — I was thinking of Ethel. I saw her face when she should know the worst; and I became, immediately, an abject, cringing, timorous thing, that crept out of the doctor's office into the spring sunshine, wondering why the world was all a-cold.

"Here's where the lash hits me: I should never have married Ethel; I should, knowing my doom, have married no one but some commonplace, platitudinous creature, whom the fortune I shall leave behind me would have consoled. But Ethel!

high-strung, ardent, simple-hearted, wor- On
shipping me far beyond my deserts! Why French-
did I condemn her, poor girl, to what is so man's
soon to come? Bay

"On the fifteenth day of the coming August, I shall have reached thirty years. Before that day, the blow will fall upon her, and it is my fault. You know, Cranbrooke, that I do not fear death. What manly soul fears death? It is only to the very young, or to the very weak of spirit, the King appears in all his terrors. Having expected him so long and so confidently, I hope I may meet him with a courageous front. But Ethel! Ethel!

"She will be quite alone with me this summer. Her mother and sisters have just sailed for the other side, and I confess I am selfish enough to crave her to myself in the last hours. But some one she must have to look after her, and whom can I trust like you? I want you to promise to come to us to spend your August holiday; to be there, in fact, when —

"In the meantime, there must be no suggestion of what I expect. She, least of all, must suspect it. I should like to

*On
French-
man's
Bay*

go out to the unknown with her light-
hearted, girlish laugh ringing in my ears.

"When we meet, as usual, you will
oblige me by saying nothing of this letter
or its contents. By complying with this
request, you will add one more — a final
one, dear old man — to the long list of
kindnesses for which I am your debtor;
and, believe me, dear Cranbrooke,

"Yours, always faithfully,

"MAXWELL POLLOCK."

"Good heaven!" exclaimed Stephen
Cranbrooke, dropping the sheet as if it
burnt him, and sitting upright and aghast.
"So *this* is the cranny in Pollock's brain
where I have never before been able to
penetrate."

Later that day, Mr. Cranbrooke received another epistle, prefaced by the
house address of the Maxwell Pollocks.

"Dear Mr. Cranbrooke," this letter
ran, "Max tells me he has extended to
you an invitation to share our solitude *à
deux* in your August holiday. I need

hardly say that I endorse this heartily; and I hope you will not regret to learn that, instead of going, as usual, to our great, big, isolated country-place in New Hampshire, I have persuaded Max to take a cottage on the shore of Frenchman's Bay, near Bar Harbor,—but not too near that gay resort,—where he can have his sail-boat and canoe, and a steam-launch for me to get about in. They say the sunsets over the water there are adorable, and Max has an artist's soul, as you know, and will delight in the picturesque beauty of it all.

"I want to tell you, confidentially, that I have fancied a change of air and scene might do him good this year. He is certainly not ill; but is, as certainly, not quite himself. I suppose you will think I am a little goose for saying so; but I believe if anything went wrong with Max, I could never stand up against it. And there is no other man in the world, than you, whom I would ask to help me to find out what it really is that worries him,—whether ill-fortune, or what,—certainly not ill-health, for he is a model of splendid vigor, as everybody knows, my beautiful husband!"

"This is what she calls pleasant reading for me," said plain, spare Stephen Cranbrooke, with a whimsical twist of his expressive mouth.

"At any rate," he read, resuming, "you and I will devote ourselves to making it nice for him up there. No man, however he loves his wife, can afford to do altogether without men's society; and it is so hard for me to get Max to go into general company, or to cultivate intimacy with any man but you!

"There is a bachelor's wing to the cottage we have taken, with a path leading direct to the wharf where the boats are moored; and this you can occupy by yourself, having breakfast alone, as Max and I are erratic in that respect. We shall have a buckboard for the ponies, and our saddle-horses, with a horse for you to ride; and we shall pledge each other not to accept a single invitation to anybody's house, unless it please us to go there.

"Not less than a month will we take

from you, and I wish it might be longer. *On* Perhaps you may like to know there is no *French-* other man Max would ask, and I should *man's* want, to be 'one of us' under such cir- *Bay* cumstances.

"Always cordially yours,
"ETHEL POLLOCK."

"I asked her for bread, and she gave me a stone," he quoted, with a return of the whimsical expression. "Well! neither he nor she has ever suspected my infatuation. I am glad she wrote as she did, though, for it makes the watch I mean to set over Max easier. After looking at his case in every aspect, I am convinced there is a remedy, if I can only find it."

A knock, just then, at the door of Mr. Cranbrooke's comfortable bachelor sitting-room was followed by the appearance inside of it of a man, at sight of whom Cranbrooke's careworn and puzzled countenance brightened perceptibly.

"Ha! Shepard!" he said, rising to bestow on the newcomer a hearty grip of the hand. "Did you divine how much I wanted to talk to a fellow who has pursued

[*153*]

exactly your line of study, and one, too, who, more than any other I happen to be acquainted with, knows just how far mind may be made to influence matter in preventing catastrophe, when — but, there, what am I to do? It's another man's affair, — a confidence that must be held inviolable."

"Give me the case hypothetically," said Shepard, dropping, according to custom, into a leathern chair out at elbows but full of comfort to the spine of reclining man, while accepting one of Cranbrooke's galaxy of famously tinted pipes.

"I think I will try to do so," rejoined his friend, "since upon it hangs the weal or woe of two people, in their way more interesting to me than any others in the world."

"I am all ears," said Dr. Shepard, fixing upon Cranbrooke the full gaze of a pair of deep-set orbs that had done their full share of looking intelligently into the mystery of cerebral vagaries. Cranbrooke, as well as he could, told the gist of Pollock's letter, expressing his opinion that to a man of the writer's temperament the conviction of approaching death was as On good as an actual death-warrant.

Shepard, who asked nothing better than man's an intelligent listener when launched upon Bay his favorite theories, kept the floor for fifteen minutes in a brilliant offhand discourse full of technicalities intermingled with sallies of strong original thought, to which Cranbrooke listened, as men in such a case are wont to do, in fascinated silence.

" But this is generalizing," the doctor interrupted himself at last. " What you want is a special discussion of your friend's condition. Of course, not knowing his physical state, I can't pretend to say how long it is likely to be before that heart-trouble will pull him up short. But the merest tyro knows that men under sentence from heart-disease have lived their full span. It is the obsession of his mind, the invasion of his nerves by that long-brooding idea, that bothers me. I am inclined to think the odds are he will go mad if he does n't die."

" Good God, Shepard !" came from his friend's pale lips.

"Isn't that what *you* were worrying about when I came in? Yes — you need n't answer. You think so, too; and we are not posing as wise men when we arrive at that simple conclusion."

"What on earth are we to do for him?"

"I don't know, unless it be to distract his mind by some utterly unlooked-for concatenation of circumstances. Get his wife to make love to another man, for instance."

"Shepard, you forget; these are my nearest friends."

"And you forget I am a sceptic about a love between the sexes that cannot be alienated," answered the little doctor, coolly.

Cranbrooke had indeed, for a moment, lost sight of his confidant's dark page of life — forgotten the experience that, years ago, had broken up the doctor's home, and made of him a scoffer against the faith of woman. He was silent, and Shepard went on with no evidence of emotion.

"When that happened to *me*, it was a dynamite explosion that effectually broke up the previous courses of thought within

me ; and, naturally, the idea occurs to me *On*
as a specific for the case of your melan- *French-*
choly friend.   Seriously, Cranbrooke, you *man's*
could do worse than attack him from some *Bay*
unexpected quarter, in some point where
he is acutely sensitive — play upon him,
excite him, distract him, and so carry him
past the date he fears."

"How could I?" asked Cranbrooke of
himself.

There was another knock; and, upon
Cranbrooke's hearty bidding to come in,
there entered no less a person than the
subject of their conversation.

Even the astute Shepard finished his
pipe and took his leave without suspecting
that the manly, healthy, clear-eyed, and
animated Maxwell Pollock had anything
in common with the possessed hero of
Cranbrooke's story. Cranbrooke, who had
dreaded a reopening of the subject of Pollock's letter, was infinitely relieved to find
it left untouched.

The visit, lasting till past midnight, was
one of a long series dating back to the time
when they were undergraduates at the uni-
versity. There had never been a break in

their friendship. The society of Cranbrooke, after that of his own wife, was to Pollock ever the most refreshing, the most inspiring to high and manly thought. They talked, now, upon topics grave and gay, without hinting at the shadow overlying all. Pollock was at his best; and his friend's heart went out to him anew in a wave of that sturdy affection " passing the love of woman " — rare, perhaps, in our material money-getting community, but, happily, still existing among true men.

When the visitor arose to take leave, he said in simple fashion : " Then I may count on you, Cranbrooke, to stand by us this summer ? "

" Count on me in all things," Cranbrooke answered; and the two shook hands, and Pollock went his way cheerily, as usual.

" Is this a dream ? " Cranbrooke asked himself, when left alone. " Can it be possible that sane, splendid fellow is a victim of pitiful hallucination, or that he is really to be cut off in the golden summer of his days. No, it can't be; it must not be. He must be, as Shepard says,

'pulled up short' by main force. At any *On*
cost, I must save him. But how? *Any-* *French-*
how! Max must be made to forget him- *man's*
self—even if I am the sacrifice! By *Bay*
George! this *is* a plight I'm in! And
Ethel, who adores the ground he walks
upon! I shall probably end by losing
both of them, worse luck!"

The morning had struggled through
Cranbrooke's window-blinds before he
stirred from his fit of musing and went
into his bedroom for a few hours of
troubled sleep.

Chapter II ·

MR. and Mrs. Pollock took possession of their summer abiding-place on a glorious day of refulgent June, such as, in the dazzling atmosphere of Mount Desert Island, makes every more southerly resort on our Atlantic coast seem dull by comparison. To greet them, they found a world of fresh-washed young birches sparkling in the sun; of spice-distilling evergreens, cropping up between gray rocks; of staring white marguerites, and huge, yellow, satin buttercups, ablow in all the clearings; of crisp, young ferns and blue iris, unfolding amid the greenery of the wilder bits of island; haunts that were soon, in turn, to be blushing pink with a miracle of brier-roses.

And what a charmed existence followed! In the morning, they awoke to see the water, beneath their windows, sparkle red in the track of the rising sun; the islets blue-black in the intense glow. All day they lived abroad in the virgin woods, or on the bay in their canoe. And, after sunsets of radiant beauty, they would fall asleep, lulled by the lapping of little waves upon the rock girdle that bound their lawn. It was all lovely, invigorating, healthful. Of the cottagers who composed the summer settlement, only those had arrived there who, like the Pollocks, wanted chiefly to be to themselves.

In these early days of the season, Max and Ethel liked to explore on horseback the bosky roads that thread the island, startling the mother partridge, crested and crafty, from her nest, or sending her, in affected woe, in a direction to lead one away from where her brood was left; lending themselves to the pretty comedy with smiles of sympathy. Or else, they would rifle the ferny combs of dew-laden blossoms, all the while hearkening to the spring chatter of birds that did their best to give utterance to what wind-voice and leaf-tone failed to convey to human comprehension. Then, emerging from green arcades, our equestrians would find themselves, now, in some rocky haunt of primeval solitude facing lonely hilltops and isolated tarns; now, gazing upon a stretch of laughing sea framed by a cleft in the highlands.

Another day, they would climb on foot to some higher mountain top, and there, whipped by tonic breezes, stand looking down upon the wooded waves of lesser summits, inland; and, seaward, to the broad Atlantic, with the ships; and, along the coast, to the hundreds of fiords, with their burden of swirling waters!

Coming home from these morning expeditions with spirit refreshed and appetite sharpened, it was their custom to repair, after luncheon, to the water, and by the aid of sails, steam, or their own oars or paddles, cut the sapphire bay with tracks of argent brightness, or linger for many a happy hour in the green shadow of the sylvan shore.

The month of July was upon the wane before husband and wife seemingly aroused to the recollection that their idyl was about to be interrupted by the invasion of a third person. Ethel, indeed, had pondered regretfully upon the coming of Cranbrooke

for some days before she spoke of it to
her husband; while Max!—

The real purpose of Cranbrooke's visit,
dismissed from Pollock's mind with extraordinary success during the earlier
weeks of their stay upon the island, had
by now assumed, in spite of him, the suggestion of a death-watch set upon a pris-
oner. He strove not to think of it. He
refrained from speaking of it. So deli-
cious had been to him the draft of Ethel's
society, uninterrupted by outsiders, in this
Eden of the eastern sea; so perfect their
harmony of thought and speech; so charming her beauty, heightened by salt air and
outdoor exercise and early hours, Max
wondered if the experience had been sent
to him as an especial allowance of mercy
to the condemned. To the very day of
Cranbrooke's arrival, even after a trap had
been sent to the evening boat to fetch him,
the husband and wife refrained from discussing the expected event.

It was the hour before sunset, following
a showery afternoon; and, standing together
upon their lawn to look at the western sky,
Max proposed to her to go out with him

[*163*]

for awhile in the canoe. They ran like children, hand in hand, to the wharf, where, lifting the frail birch-bark craft from its nest, he set it lightly afloat. Ethel, stepping expertly into her place, was followed by Max, who, in his loose cheviot shirt, barearmed and bareheaded, flashing his red-dyed paddle in the clear water, seemed to her the embodiment of manly grace and strength.

They steered out into the bay; and, as they paused to look back upon the shore, the glory of the scene grew to be unspeakable. Behind the village, over which the electric globes had not yet begun to gleam, towered Newport, a rampart of glowing bronze, arched by a rainbow printed upon a brooding cloud. Elsewhere, the multicolored sky flamed with changing hues, reflected in a sea of glass. And out of this sea arose wooded islands; and, far on the opposite shore of the mainland, the triple hills had put on a vestment of deepest royal purple.

"I like to look away from the splendor, to the side that is in shadow," said Ethel. "See, along that eastern coast, how the

reflected sunlight is flashed from the win- *On*
dows on that height, and the blue columns *French-*
of hearth smoke arise from the chimneys! *man's*
Does n't it make you somehow rejoice *Bay*
that, when the color fades, as it soon must,
we shall still have our home and the lights
we make for ourselves to go back to?"

There was a long silence.

"What has set you to moralizing,
dear?" he asked, trying to conceal that
he had winced at her innocent question.

"Oh! nothing. Only, when one is su-
premely happy, as I am now, one is afraid
to believe it will endure. How mild the
air is to-night! Look over yonder, Max;
the jewelled necklace of Sorrento's lights
has begun to palpitate. Let us paddle
around that fishing-schooner before we
turn."

" Ethel, you are crying."

" Am I? Then it is for pure delight.
I think, Max, we had never so fine an
inspiration as that of coming to Mount
Desert. My idea of the place has always
been of a lot of rantipole gaieties, and people crowded in hotels. While this — it is
a little like Norway, and a great deal like

Southern Italy.   Besides, when before
have we been so completely to ourselves
as in that gray stone lodge by the waterside, with its hood of green ivy, and the
green hill rising behind it ?   Let us come
every year ; better still, let us build ourselves a summer home upon these shores."

"Should you like me to buy the cottage
we now have, so that you can keep it to
come to when you like ? "

"When *you* like, you mean.   Max, it
can't be you have caught cold in this soft
air, but your voice sounds a little hoarse.
Well !   I suppose we must go in, for Mr.
Cranbrooke will be arriving very soon."

Ethel's sigh found an echo in one from
her husband, at which the April-natured
young woman laughed.

"There, it's out ! We don't want even
Cranbrooke, do we ?   To think the poor,
dear man's coming should have been op-
pressing both of us, and neither would be
first to acknowledge it !   After all, Max
darling, it is your fault.   It was you who
proposed Cranbrooke.   I knew, all along,
that I 'd be better satisfied with you alone.
Now, we must just take the consequence

of your overhasty hospitality, and make him as happy as we are — if we can."

"If we can!" said Max; and she saw an almost pathetic expression drift across his face — an expression that bewildered her.

"Why do you look so rueful over him?"

"I am thinking, perhaps, how hard it will be for him to look at happiness through another man's eyes."

"Nonsense! Mr. Cranbrooke is quite satisfied with his own lot. He is one of those self-contained men who could never really love, I think," said Mrs. Pollock, conclusively.

"He has in some way failed to show you his best side. He has the biggest, tenderest heart! I wish there was a woman fit for him, somewhere. But Stephen will never marry, now, I fear. She who gets him will be lucky — he is a very tower of strength to those who lean on him."

"As far as strength goes, Max, you could pick him up with your right hand. It may be silly, but I do love your size and vigor; when I see you in a crowd of average men, I exult in you. Imagine any woman who could get *you* wanting a thin, sallow person like Cranbrooke!"

"He can be fascinating, when he chooses," said Max.

"The best thing about Cranbrooke, Max, is that he loves you," answered his wife, wilfully.

"Then I want you, henceforth, to try to like him better, dear; to like him for himself. He is coming in answer to my urgent request; and I feel certain the more you know of him, the more you will trust in him. At any rate, give him as much of your dear self as I can spare, and you will be sure of pleasing me."

"Max, now I believe it is you who are crying because you are too happy. I never heard such a solemn cadence in your voice. I don't want a minute of this lovely time to be sad. When we were in town, I fancied you were down — about something; now, you are yourself again; let me be happy without alloy. I am determined to be the *cigale* of the French fable, and dance and sing away the summer. Between us, we may even succeed in making that sober Cranbrooke a reflection of us both. There, now, the light has faded; quicken your speed; we must go ashore and meet him. See, the moon has risen — O Max darling, to please me, paddle in that silver path!"

This was the Ethel her husband liked best to see, — a child in her quick variations of emotion, a woman in steadfast tenderness. Conquering his own strongly excited feeling, he smiled on her indulgently; and when, their landing reached, Cranbrooke's tall form was descried coming down the bridge to receive them, he was able to greet his friend with an unshadowed face.

The three went in to dinner, which Ethel, taking advantage of the soft, dry air, had ordered to be served in a *loggia* opening upon the water. The butler, a sympathetic Swede, had decked their little round table with wild roses in shades of shell-pink, deepening to crimson. The candles, burning under pale-green shades, were scarcely stirred by the faint breeze. Hard, indeed, to believe that, upon occasion, that couchant monster, the bay, could break up into huge waves, ramping shore-

[*169*]

ward, leaping over the rock wall, upon the lawn, up to the *loggia* floor, and there beat for admission to the house, upon storm-shutters hastily erected to meet its onslaught!

To-night, a swinging lantern of wrought iron sent down through its panels of opal glass a gentle illumination upon three well-pleased faces gathered around the dainty little feast. Ethel, who, in the days of gipsying, would allow no toilets of ceremony, retained her sailor-hat, with the boat-gown of white serge, in which her infantile beauty showed to its best advantage. Cranbrooke was dazzled by the new bloom upon her face, the new light in her eye.

Pollock, too, tall, broad-shouldered, blonde, clean-shaven save for a mustache, his costume of white flannel enhancing duly the transparent healthiness of his complexion, looked wonderfully well — so Cranbrooke thought and said.

"Does he not?" cried Ethel, exultingly. "I knew you would think so. Max has been reconstructed since we have lived outdoors in this wonderful air. Just

wait, Mr. Cranbrooke, till we have done
with you, and you, too, will be blossom- *French-*
ing like the rose." *man's*

"I, that was a desert, you would say," *Bay*
returned Cranbrooke, smiling. Involun-
tarily it occurred to him to contrast his
own outer man with that of his host.
Somehow or other, the fond, satisfied look
Ethel bestowed upon her lord aroused
anew in their friend an old, teasing spirit
of envy of nature's bounty to another,
denied to him.

As the moon transmuted to silver the
stretch of water east of them, and the three
sat over the table, with its *carafes* and de-
canters and egg-shell coffee-cups, till the
flame of a cigar-lighter died utterly in its
silver beak, their talk touching all subjects
pleasantly, Cranbrooke persuaded himself
he had indeed been dreaming a bad
dream. The journey thither, of which
every mile had been like the link of a
chain, was, for him, after all, a mere essay
at pleasure-seeking. He had come on to
spend a jolly holiday with a couple of the
nicest people in the world — nothing more!
His fancies, his plans, his devices, con-

[*171*]

ceived in sore distress of spirit, were relegated to the world of shadows, whence they had been summoned.

When Ethel left the two men for the night, and the butler came out to collect his various belongings, Pollock rose and bade Cranbrooke accompany him to see the mountains from the other side of the house. Here, turning their backs on the enchantment of the water view, they looked up at an amphitheatre of hills, dominated in turn by rocky summits gleaming in the moon. But for the lap of the water upon the coast, the stir of a fresh wind arising to whisper to the leaves of a clump of birches, Mother Earth around them was keeping silent vigil.

"What a perfect midsummer night!" said Cranbrooke, drawing a deep breath of enjoyment. "After the heat and dust of that three hundred miles of railway journey from Boston, this *is* a reward!"

"We chose better than we knew the scene of my euthanasia," answered Pollock, without a tremor in his voice.

A thrill ran through Cranbrooke's veins. He could have sworn the air had suddenly become chill, as if an iceberg had floated into the bay. He tried to respond, and found himself babbling words of weak conventionality; and all the while the soul of the strong man within him was saying: "It must not be. It shall not be. If I live, I shall rescue you from this ghastly phantom."

"Don't think it necessary to give words to what you feel for me," said Pollock, smiling slightly. "You are not making a brilliant success of it, old man, and you'd better stop. And don't suppose I mean to continue to entertain my guest by lugubrious discussions of my approaching *finale*. Only, it is necessary that you should know several things, since the event may take us unawares. I have made you my executor, and Ethel gets all there is; that's the long and short of my will, properly signed, attested, and deposited with my lawyer before I left town. Ethel's mother and sisters will be returning to Newport in a fortnight, and they will, no doubt, come to the poor child when she needs them. There *must* be some compensation for a decree of this kind, and I have it in the absolute bliss I have enjoyed since we came here. That child-wife of mine is the most enchanting creature in the world. If I were not steeped in selfishness, I could wish she loved me a little less. But all emotions pass, and even Ethel's tears will dry."

" Good Heaven, Max, you are talking like a machine ! One would think this affair of yours certain. Who are you, to dare to penetrate the mystery of the decrees of your Maker — "

" None of that, if you please, Cranbrooke," interrupted Pollock; " I have fought every inch of the way along there, by myself, and have been conquered by my conviction. Did I tell you that my father, before me, struggled with similar remonstrances from *his* friends ? The parsons even brought bell and book to exorcise his tormentor — and all in vain. He was snuffed out in full health, as I shall be, and why should I whine at following him ? Come, my dear fellow, I am keeping you out of a capital bed, from sleep you must require. There's but one matter in which you can serve me, — take Ethel

into your care. Win her fullest confidence; let her know that when I am not
there, *you will be*."

Cranbrooke went to his room, but not
to rest. When his friends next saw him,
he was returning from a solitary cruise
about the bay in a catboat Pollock kept
at anchor near their wharf.

"Why, Mr. Cranbrooke!" cried Ethel,
lightly. "The boatman says you have
been out ever since daybreak. But that
we espied the boat tacking about beyond
that far rock, I should have been for sending in search of you."

"Cranbrooke is an accomplished sailor,"
said Max. "But just now, breakfast's
the thing for him, Ethel. See that he is
well fed, while I stroll out to the stable
and look after the horses."

As he crossed the greensward, Ethel's
gaze followed him, till he disappeared behind a clump of trees. Then she turned
to her guest.

"Let me serve you with all there is,
until they bring you something hot," she
said, with her usual half-flippant consideration of him. "Do you know you look

very seedy? I have, for my part, no patience with these early morning exploits."

"If you could have seen the world awakening as I saw it, this morning, you would condone my offence," he answered, a curious expression Ethel thought she had detected in his eyes leaving them unclouded, as he spoke.

Chapter III

NO one who knew Stephen Cranbrooke well could say he did anything by halves. In the days that followed his arrival at Mount Desert, Max Pollock saw that his friend was lending every effort to the task of establishing friendly relations with his wife. From her first half-petulant, half-cordial manner with him, — the manner of a woman who tries to please her husband by recognition of the claim of his nearest male intimate, — Ethel had passed to the degree of manifestly welcoming Cranbrooke's presence, both when with her husband and without him.

As Max saw this growing friendship, he strove to increase it by absenting himself from Ethel, instead of, as heretofore, spending every hour he could wring from the society of other folk, in the light of her smiles. His one wish that Ethel

On Frenchman's Bay

[*177*]

might be insensibly led to find another than himself companionable; that she might be, though never so little, weaned from her absolute dependence upon him for daily happiness, before the blow fell that was to plunge her in darkest night, kept him content in these acts of self-sacrifice.

But, as was inevitable, his manner toward them both underwent a trifling change. His old buoyancy of affection was succeeded by a quiet, at times wistful, recognition of the fact that his friend and his wife had now found another interest besides himself. But he was proud to see Cranbrooke had justified his boast that he " could be fascinating when he chose ; " and he was glad to think Cranbrooke at last realized the charm Ethel, apparently a mere bright bubble upon the tide of society, had to a man of intellect and heart. " It was as I said," the poor fellow repeated to himself, trying to find comfort in the realization of his prescience; and when Ethel, alone with him, would break into pæans of his friend, and wonder how she could have been so blind to the " real man " before, Max answered her loyally that his highest wish for both of them was at last gratified.

Then the day came when there was question of a companion for Ethel in a sailing-party to which she had accepted an invitation — and for Max was destined an emotion something like distaste.

They were sitting over the breakfast table, — a meal no longer exclusive to wife and husband, as had been agreed, but shared by Cranbrooke with due regularity, — when Ethel broached the subject.

" You know, Max, I was foolish enough to promise that irresistible Mrs. Clayton — when she would not take no for an answer, yesterday, — that *some* of us would join her water party to-day. It is to be an idle cruise, with no especial aim — luncheon on board their schooner-yacht; the sort of thing I knew would bore you to extinction — being huddled up with the same people half the day."

" It is the opening wedge — if you go to this, you will be booked for others, that's all," said Max, preparing to say, in a martyrized way, that he would accompany her, if she liked.

[*179*]

"Oh, I knew you would feel that; and so I told her she must really excuse my husband, but that I had no doubt Mr. Cranbrooke would accept with pleasure. You see, Mr. Cranbrooke, what polite inaccuracies you are pledged by friendship to sustain."

"I *will* go with pleasure," Stephen said, with what Max thought almost unnecessary readiness.

"Bravo!" cried Ethel. "This is the hero's spirit. And so, Max dear, you will have a long day to yourself while I am experimenting in fashionable pleasuring, and Mr. Cranbrooke is representing you in keeping an eye on me."

"You will, of course, be at home to dinner?" said her husband.

"Surely. Unless breezes betray us, and we are driven to support exhausted nature upon hardtack and champagne; for, of course, all of the Claytons' luncheon will be eaten up, and there are no stores aboard a craft like that. Will you order the buckboard for ten, dear? We rendezvous at the boat-wharf. And, as there is no telling when we shall be in, don't trouble

to send to meet me. Mr. Cranbrooke and
I will pick up a trap to return in."

Max saw them off in the buckboard;
and, as Ethel turned at some little distance and looked back at him, where he
still stood on the gravel before their vine-
wreathed portal, waving her hand with a
charming grace, then settling again to a
tête-à-tête with Cranbrooke, he felt vaguely
resentful at being left behind.

The clear, dazzling atmosphere, the
sense of youthful vitality in his being,
made him repel the idea of exclusion from
any function of the animated world. He
almost thought Ethel should have given
him a chance to say whether or no he
would accompany her. Was it not, upon
her part, even a little bit — a *very* little bit,
lacking in proper wifely feeling, to be so
prompt in dispensing with his society, to
accept that of others for a whole, long,
bright summer's day of pleasuring?

This suggestion he put away from him
as quickly as it came. He was like a
spoiled child, he said to himself, who does
not expect to be taken at his word. Ethel
well knew his dislike of gossiping groups

of idle people; equally well she remembered, no doubt, his frequent requests that she would mingle more with the world, take more pleasure on her own account. And Cranbrooke,—dear old Cranbrooke, —of course he was ready to punish himself by going off on such a party, when it was an opportunity to serve his friend!

So Max put his discontent away, and, mounting his horse, went off alone for a ride half around the island, lunching at Northeast Harbor, and returning, through devious ways, by nightfall.

Restored to healthy enjoyment of all things by his day in the saddle, he turned into the avenue leading to their house, buoyed up by the sweet hope of Ethel returned — Ethel on the watch for him. Already, he saw in fancy the gleam of her jaunty white yachting-costume between the tubs of flowering hydrangeas ranged on either side the walk before their door. The lamps inside — the " home lights," of which she had once fondly spoken to him — were already lighted. She would, perhaps, be worrying at his delay. He quickened his speed, and rode down the avenue

to the house at a brisk trot.   The groom, *On*
who, from the stable, had heard the horse's *French-*
feet, started up out of the shrubbery to *man's*
meet him.   But there was no other indi- *Bay*
cation of a watch upon the movements of
the master of the house.

" Mrs. Pollock has not returned, then ? "
he asked, conscious of blankness in his
tone.

" No, sir; not yet.   Our orders were,
not to send for her, sir, as there was no
knowing when the party would get in."

" Yes, the breeze has pretty much died
out since sunset," said Pollock, endeavor-
ing to mask his disappointment by commonplace.

He went indoors; and the house, care-
fully arranged though it was, with flowers
and furniture disposed by expert hands to
greet the returning of the master, seemed
to him dull and chill.   He ordered a cup
of tea for himself, and, bending down, put
a match to the little fire of birch-wood
always kept laid upon the hearth of their
picturesque hall sitting-room.

In a moment, the curling wreathes of
pale azure that arose upon the pyre of

silvery-barked logs was succeeded by a generous flame. The peculiarly sweet flavor of the burning birch was distilled upon the air. Sipping the cup of tea, as he stood in his riding-clothes before the fire, Max felt a consoling warmth invade his members and expand his heart.

"They will be in directly," he said; "and, by George, I shall be as ready for my dinner as they for theirs."

In one corner of the hall stood a tall, slender-necked vase, where he had that morning watched Ethel arranging a sheaf of goldenrod with brown-seeded marsh-grasses, — a combination her touch had made individual and artistic to a striking degree. He recalled how, as she had finished it, she looked around, calling him and Stephen from their newspapers to admire her handiwork. He, the husband, had admired it lazily from his divan of cushions in the corner. Cranbrooke had gone over to stand beside his hostess, and thence they had passed, still in close conversation, out to the grassy terrace above the sea.

Now, why should this recollection

awaken in Max Pollock a new sense of *On*
the feeling he had been doing his best to *French-*
dispose of all day? He could not say; *man's*
but there it was, to prick him with its in- *Bay*
visible sting. Then, too, the dinner-hour
was past, and he was hungry.

He went out upon the veranda at the
rear, and surveyed the expanse of water.
Far off, between the electric ball that hung
over the wharf of the village, and the point
of Bar Island, opposite, he saw a bridge of
lights from yachts of all sorts, with which
the harbor was now full. He fancied a
little moving star of light, that seemed to
creep beneath the large ones, might be the
Claytons' boat on her return, and, after
another interval of watching, called up a
wharf authority by telephone, and asked
if the *Lorelei* was in.

" Not yet, sir," was the reply. " Probably caught out when the wind fell. Will
let you know the minute they are in sight."
With which assurance Mr. Pollock was
finally driven by the pangs of natural appetite to sit down alone to a cheerless meal.

There was a message by telephone, as
he finished his repast. The *Lorelei* was

r

in, and Mrs. Pollock desired to speak with her husband.

"We're all right," Ethel's voice said, "and I hope you have n't been worried. They *insist* on our going to dinner at a restaurant, and, of course, you understand, I can't spoil the fun by refusing. *Could n't* you come down and meet us?"

His first impulse was to say yes; but a second thought withheld him. He gave her a pleasant answer, however, bidding her enjoy herself without thought of him, and adding: "Cranbrooke will look out for you and bring you home."

It was quite ten o'clock when they arrived at the cottage, Ethel in high spirits, flushed with the excitement of a merry day, full of chatter over people and things Max had no interest in, appealing to Cranbrooke to enjoy her retrospects with her. She was "awfully sorry" about having kept Max from his dinner; "awfully sorry" not to have come home at once, but there was no getting out of the impromptu dinner; and, of course, they had to wait for it; and she was

[*186*]

the first, after dinner, to ma *On*
to go; Mr. Cranbrooke wou .ty to *French-*
that. *man's*

"I don't need any certification, dear," *Bay*
said Max, gently; but he did not smile.
Cranbrooke, who sat with him after sleepy
Ethel had retired from the scene, felt his
heart wrung at thought of certain things
that never entered into Ethel's little head.
But he made no effort to dispel the cloud
that had settled over his friend's face.

By and by, Cranbrooke, too, said good-
night, and went off into his wing, and Max
was left alone with his cigar.

The day on the water had verified
Max's prediction that it would prove "an
opening wedge." Ethel, caught in the
tide of the season's gaieties, found herself
impelled from one entertainment to the
other; their cottage was invaded by call-
ers, their little informal dinners were
transformed into banquets of ceremony, as
choice and more lively than those of their
conventional life in town. The only persons really satisfied by the change of habits in the house were the servants, who,

[*187*]

like all artists, require a public to set the seal upon their worth.

Max, bewildered, found himself some-times accompanying his wife to her par-ties; oftener — struck with the ghastly inappropriateness of his presence in such haunts — stopping at home and deputing to Cranbrooke the escort of his wife. To his surprise, he perceived that Cranbrooke was not only ready, but eager, on all occa-sions, to carry Ethel away from him. But then, of course, this was precisely what he had wished.

And Ethel, who lost no opportunity to tell Max how "good," how "lovely," Cranbrooke had been to her, was she not carrying out to the letter her husband's wishes? He observed, moreover, that Ethel was even more impressed than he had expected her to be with that quality of "fascination." Cranbrooke's mind was like a beautiful new country into which she was making excursions, she said once; and Max, after a moment's hesitation, agreed with her very warmly.

At last, Maxwell Pollock awoke one morning, with a start of disagreeable con-

sciousness, to the fact that this was the eve
of his thirtieth birthday. Occupied as he *French-*
had been with various thoughts that had to *man's*
do with his transient relations to this *Bay*
sublunary sphere, he had actually allowed
himself to lose sight of the swift approach
of his day of doom. Now, he arose, took
his bath, dressed, and without arousing his
wife, who, in the room adjoining, slept
profoundly after a gay dance overnight,
went alone to the waterside, with the intention of going out in his canoe.

Early as he was, Cranbrooke was before him, carrying the canoe upon his
head, moving after the fashion of some
queer shelled-creature down to the float.

Max realized, with a sense of keen self-
rebuke, that the spectacle of his friend
was repellant to him, and the prospect of
a talk alone with Stephen on this occasion, the last thing he would have chosen.

And — evidently a part of the latter-
day revolution of affairs — Cranbrooke
seemed to have forgotten that this day
meant more than another to Pollock. He
greeted him cheerily, in commonplace
terms, commented on their identity of

fancy in the matter of a paddle at sunrise, and offered to relinquish the craft in favor of its owner.

" Of course not. Get in, will you," said Max, throwing off his coat; and, taking one of the paddles, while Cranbrooke plied the other, their swift, even strokes soon carried them far over toward the illuminated east.

When well out upon the bay, they paused to watch the red coming of the sun. Beautiful with matin freshness was the sleeping world around them; and, inspired by the scene, Max, who was kneeling in the bow, turned to exclaim to Cranbrooke, with his old, hearty voice, upon the reward coming to early risers in such surroundings.

" Jove, a man feels born again when he breathes air like this ! "

Cranbrooke started. It was almost beyond hope that Max should use such a phrase, in such accents, at such a juncture. Immediately, however, the exhilaration died out of Pollock's manner; and, again turning away his face, he showed that his thoughts had reverted to the old sore spot.

He did not see the expression of almost *On* womanly yearning in Cranbrooke's face *French-* when the certainty of this was fixed upon *man's* his anxious mind. *Bay*

The two men talked little, and of casual things only, while abroad. As they returned to the house, Cranbrooke made a movement as if to speak out something burning upon his tongue, and then, repressing it, walked with hasty strides to his own apartment.

The day passed as had done those immediately preceding it. Calls, a party of guests at luncheon, a drive, absorbed Ethel's hours from her husband. When she reached home, at tea-time, he had come in from riding, and was standing alone in the hall, awaiting her.

"How nice to find you here alone!" she cried, going up to kiss him, and then taking her place behind the tea-tray. "Do sit down, and let us imagine we are back in those dear old days before we were overpowered by outsiders. Never mind! The rush will soon be over; we shall be to ourselves again, you and I and — how stupid I am!" she added, coloring.

[*191*]

"You and I, I mean, for he must go back to town."

"You mean Cranbrooke?" he said, as she thought, absent-mindedly, but in reality with something like a cold hand upon his heart, that for a moment gave him a sense of physical apprehension. Had *it* come, he wondered?

But no, this was not physical; this was a shock of purely emotional displeasure. Could he believe his ears, that Ethel, his wife, had indeed blended another than himself with her dream of returning solitude?

"Yes, it will be all over soon," he said, mechanically. "Had you a pleasant drive? And did you enjoy the box-seat with Egmont?"

"Oh! Egmont, fortunately, can drive —if he *can't* talk," she answered, lightly. "I suppose I am fastidious, or else spoiled for the conversation of ordinary men, after what I have had recently from Cranbrooke. By the way, Max dear, are you relentless against going with us to-night, to the *fête* at the canoe club? You need n't go in-

[*192*]

side the club-house, you know. It will be lovely to look at, from the water."

"With *us*? Then Cranbrooke has already promised?"

"Yes, of course; he could not leave me in the lurch, could he, when my husband is such an obstinate recluse?"

"And how do you intend to get there?"

"By water, stupid, of course; how else? I will be satisfied with the rowboat, if you won't trust me in the canoe; but Mr. Cranbrooke is such an expert with the paddle, I should n't think you would object to letting me go with him. It will be perfectly smooth water, and the air is so mild. Do say I may go in the canoe, dear; it's twice the fun."

"I think you know that, unless I take you, it is my wish you go nowhere at night in a canoe," he answered, coldly.

Ethel was more hurt at his tone than disappointed by his refusal. She could not think what had come over her husband, of late, so often had this constrained manner presented itself to her advance. She set it down to her unwonted indulgence

[*193*]

in society, and promised herself, with a sigh of relinquishment, that, after this summer, she would go back to her life lived for Max alone.

Then, Cranbrooke coming in with two or three visitors, who lingered till almost dinner-time and were persuaded easily to stop for dinner, there was no chance to indulge in meditations, penitential or otherwise. When her guests took their departure, it was in the little steam-launch, she and Cranbrooke accompanying the party, and all bound for the *fête*, to be given on a wooded island in the bay. As they were leaving the house, something impelled her to run back and, in the semi-darkness of the veranda, seek her husband's side.

"Max darling, kiss me good-by. Or, if you want me, let me stay with you."

"No, no; I want you to enjoy every moment while you can," he said, withdrawing from her gaze to the shadow of a vine-wreathed column.

"Max, your voice is strange. And once, at dinner, I saw you looking at me, and there was something in your eyes that

frightened me. If you had n't smiled, and
lifted your glass to pledge me, I should
not have known what to think."

"Ethel! Wife! Do you love me?" he
said, catching her to his heart.

"Max! Why, Max! You foolish boy,
we shall be seen."

"Tell me, and I iss me once more, my
own, my own!"

"They are all aboard except you, Mrs.
Pollock," a voice said; and, from the dew
of the lawn, Cranbrooke stepped upon the
veranda.

Max started violently, and let his wife
go from his embrace.

"You see how rude you are making me
toward our guests," said Ethel. "You
have my wrap, Mr. Cranbrooke? Good-
night, Max; and to-morrow I'll tell you
all about it. Better change your mind
and come after us, though."

"Max need not trouble to do so," put
in Cranbrooke, in a muffled voice. "As
usual, I will fill his place."

Max thought he almost hurried her
away. They went down the slope of the
lawn together; and, at the steep descent

leading to the bridge, he saw Ethel stumble, and Cranbrooke throw his arm around her to steady her.

And now, a passion took possession of Maxwell Pollock's being that impelled him to the impetuous action of following them to the wharf, and gesticulating madly after the swift little steamer that bore them away from him.

"He dared take her, did he, when she would have stayed at a word from me? I see all, now. Specious, false, damnably false, he has snared her fancy in his net. But she loves me, I'll swear she loves me, and I'll snatch her from him, if it is with the last effort of my strength. Is there time? Well, what is to come, let it come! While there's life in me, she is mine."

A moment, and he was afloat in the canoe, no sign of weakness in his powerful stroke with the paddle, no thought in his brain but the one intense determination of the male creature to wrest his beloved from the hands of his rival.

Every one conceded this to be quite the prettiest and most taking event of the season. The rustic club-house, its peaked gable and veranda defined with strings of colored lanterns, sent forth the music of a band, while to its portal trooped maidens and cavaliers, landing at the wharf from every variety of craft. The woods behind were linked with chains of light, the shore below lit with bonfires, and more evanescent eruptions of many-hued fireworks. Rockets hissed through the air, and broke in a rain of violet, green, and crimson meteors, till the zenith was a tangled mesh made by the trails of them; fireballoons arose and were lost among the stars; little fire-boats, launched from vessels stocked for the purpose, bore their blazing cargoes out upon the tide; other unnamed monsters were let loose to carry apparent destruction zigzag through the waves. Every attendant yacht, sloop, launch, rowboat, or canoe, with which the water about the island was covered, carried quaint decoration in the guise of Chinese lanterns. Some of the smaller boats were arched with these; others tossed bouquets of fiery bubbles into the air. Creeping about at a snail's pace among the crowded boats, invisible canoes carried silent passengers; an occasional " oh ! " of exclamation at the beauty of the scene, the only contribution people felt inclined to make to conversation. It was a pageant of bedazzlement, as if witches, gnomes, spirits of earth, air, and the underworld, had mingled their resources to enchant the eyes of mortals. And over all, sailed the lady-moon serenely, forgotten, but sure that her time would come again.

Max found his launch without difficulty, on the outer circle of the amphitheatre of light. As he had divined, it was empty, save for the two boatmen.

" The ladies went ashore, sir," one of his men said, in answer to his inquiry. " All but Mrs. Pollock, sir."

" Mrs. Pollock ? Where is she, then ? " he asked, briefly.

" She took our rowboat, sir, and went off on the water with one of the gentlemen. Mr. Cranbrooke, I think it was; and they ordered us to wait just here. No good going ashore, sir, if you want to see. It 's better from this point, even, than nearer in."

[*198*]

"Very well," said the master, and at once his canoe moved off to be lost in the crowd.

He had sought for them in vain, peering into all the small boats whenever the flash-light of the rockets, or the catharine-wheels on the coast, lit the scene. Many a tender interlude was thus revealed; but of the two people he now longed with the fever of madness to discover, he saw nothing.

At last, in a burst from a candle rocket, there was a glimpse of Ethel's red boat-cloak, her bare, golden head rising above it. She was sitting in the stern of the rowboat, Cranbrooke beside her, their bow above water, their oars negligently trailing. Ethel's eyes were fixed upon the glittering panorama; but Cranbrooke's eyes were riveted on her.

With an oath, Max drove his paddle fiercely into the sea. The canoe sped forward like an arrow. Blind with anger, he did not observe that he was directly in the track of a little steamer laden with new arrivals, turning in toward the wharf.

A new day dawned before the doctors, who had been all night battling for Maxwell Pollock's life, left him restored to consciousness, and reasonably secure of carrying no lasting ill effect from the blow on his head received by collision with the steamer.

Carried under with his canoe, he had arisen to full view in the glare from a " set piece " of fireworks on the shore, beside the boat containing Cranbrooke and his wife. It was Cranbrooke, not Ethel, who identified the white face coming to the surface within reach of his hand, then sinking again out of sight. It was Cranbrooke, also, who sprang to Pollock's rescue, and, floating with his inert body, was dragged with him aboard the launch.

As the rosy light of the east came to play upon Pollock's features, he opened his eyes for the first time with a look of intelligence. At his bedside, Ethel was kneeling, her whole loving soul in her gaze.

" Is this — I thought it was heaven," he said, feeling for her hand.

" It is heaven for me, now that I have

you back, my own darling," she answered,
through happy tears.

" Have I been here long ? "

" A few hours since the accident. The
doctors say you will be none the worse
for it. And, Max dear, only think! This
is your birthday! Your thirtieth birthday! Many, many, *many* happy returns!"
and she punctuated her wish with warm
kisses.

At that juncture, Cranbrooke came into
the room and stood at the side of the bed
opposite Ethel, who had no eyes for him,
but kept on gazing at her recovered treasure as if she could never have enough.

Max, though aware of Stephen's presence, made no movement of recognition,
till Ethel spoke in playful chiding.

" Darling! Where are your manners ?
Are n't you going to speak to our friend,
and thank him for saving you — saving
you for *me*, thank God!"

She buried her face in the bed-clothes,
overcome with the recollection; but even
with the exquisite tenderness of her accents thrilling in his ear, Max remained
obstinately dumb to Stephen Cranbrooke.

On French-man's Bay

"Forgive him; he is not himself!" pleaded Ethel, as she saw Cranbrooke about to go dejectedly out of the room.

"Some day he will understand me," answered Stephen, with a gallant effort at self-control. Then, withdrawing, he murmured to himself: "But he will never know that, in playing with his edged tools, it is I who have got the death-blow."